AF413684

CATHOLIC FEAST DAYS

CATHOLIC FEAST DAYS

A COOKBOOK FOR CONNECTING FAITH AND FOOD

ALEXANDRA GREELEY

SOPHIA INSTITUTE PRESS
Manchester, NH

Sophia Institute Press
Box 5284, Manchester, NH 03108
1-800-888-9344
www.SophiaInstitute.com

Sophia Institute Press® is a registered trademark of Sophia Institute.

paperback ISBN 979-8-88911-310-2

ebook ISBN 979-8-88911-311-9

Library of Congress Control Number: 2025945994

First printing

Contents

CHRISTMAS SEASON

ORDINARY TIME: BETWEEN CHRISTMAS AND LENT

LENT

HOLY WEEK

EASTER SEASON

ORDINARY TIME: BETWEEN PENTECOST AND ADVENT

CATHOLIC FEAST DAYS

Introduction
Living (and Cooking) Liturgically

For the Church, time is more than dates and seasons—it's a sacred rhythm, an invitation to journey with Christ through His life, death, and Resurrection. The liturgical year is the Church's way of helping us sanctify time, offering a pattern of seasons and feast days that call us not only to remember and reflect, but also to participate and be drawn into the saving mysteries of the Faith.

Beginning with Advent, we wait in hope and perform acts of penance to prepare our hearts for Christ's coming—both in Bethlehem and at the end of time. Christmas follows in a burst of joy, celebrating the birth of our Savior, the Light of the world. Then comes Ordinary Time—not dull or mundane, but "ordered time," where we walk alongside Jesus in His earthly ministry, learning from His words and deeds. Lent draws us back into penance and preparation, as we journey with Christ into His Passion and death. Once the faithful have died with Christ during Lent, they are brought to the glory and joys of His Resurrection in the Easter season. Pentecost then ignites the Church with the fire of the Holy Spirit, and we return once more to Ordinary Time, our hearts set on the Kingdom to come.

Throughout the liturgical year, the Church uses the material world to communicate the sacred—from the Nativity scenes of Advent and Christmas to the ashes of Ash Wednesday. However, these sacred encounters need not be limited to liturgical rites alone. Families can and should bring the liturgy into their homes to sanctify their daily routine and draw them into the mysteries that the liturgical seasons communicate.

And what better way to mark these moments than around the family table? There's a reason why the Church has such a storied culinary tradition that spans across time and cultures. The plentitude of feasts, fasts, and festivals in the Church's calendar provide ample opportunities for families and communities to live out and enter into the Church's life together. This cookbook aims to offer the faithful a sampling of the Church's liturgical culinary traditions so that families can better experience now what they will in eternity. We also aim to dress up the table to reflect the Church's liturgical colors and symbols (please see Appendix II for liturgically themed place cards).

For, in the words of the *Catechism of the Catholic Church*, the liturgy is "an 'action' of the *whole Christ (Christus totus)*" (*CCC* 1136), that which we celebrate now in sign and in fullness in the world to come.

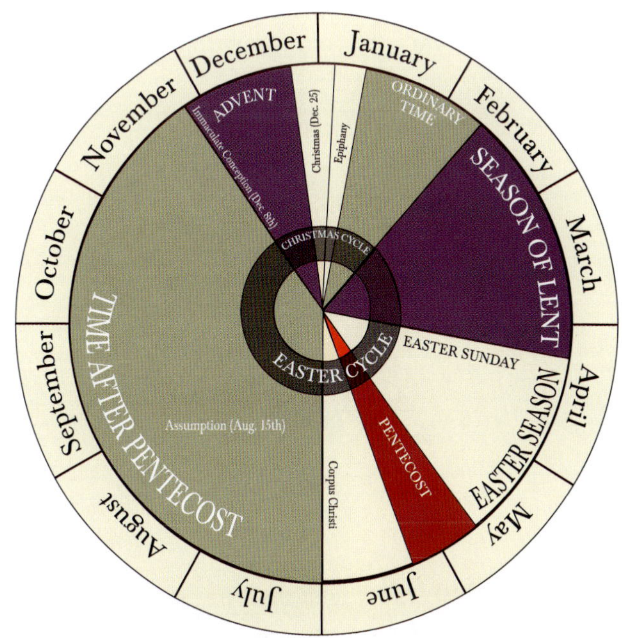

Let Us Pray

O come, O come, Emmanuel,
And ransom captive Israel,
That mourns in lonely exile here,
Until the Son of God appear.
Rejoice! Rejoice! Emmanuel
Shall come to thee, O Israel.

ADVENT

The word *Advent* derives from the Latin word *adventus*, or "coming." Advent likely began in the fourth century as a period of fasting and preparation for Epiphany. In the sixth century, St. Gregory the Great linked the Advent season with the coming of Christ. But historians say there is more to what the Advent season means. Advent was a season of preparation for new Christians during the feast of Epiphany. Advent also celebrated the baptism of Christ in the Jordan River and Christ's first miracle at Cana.

By the Middle Ages, four Sundays had become the accepted length of Advent. During this period, Christians would spend those days in penance and fasting. The Church also taught that Advent's meaning included the coming of Christ in Bethlehem, His future coming at the end of times, and His presence through the promised Holy Spirit. For Western Christian denominations, Advent begins on the fourth Sunday before Christmas, and it marks the beginning of the liturgical year. The Advent season lasts through Christmas Eve.

The Advent season is a time of joyful expectation, a sacred period of waiting and preparation for the coming of Christ. But for centuries, it has also been a time of rich culinary traditions that reflect the spiritual rhythms of the Church. From the early Christians who fasted in anticipation of Christmas to medieval monks who prepared humble yet hearty meals for the season, food has always played a central role in marking the sacred days of Advent.

Even in simplicity, families found ways to celebrate. Feast days of beloved saints—St. Nicholas, St. Barbara, and Our Lady of Guadalupe, to name a few—brought moments of joyful indulgence with treats like baklava, sweet breads, and *mole*.

JESSE TREE ORNAMENTS

What is a Jesse Tree? The name first appears in the book of Isaiah, which says, "There shall come forth a shoot from the stump of Jesse, and a branch shall grow out of his roots" (Isa. 11:1). The link between Jesse and Jesus Christ is clear: Jesse was the father of King David, and Christ descended from that line.

A Jesse Tree can take many forms: a real tree, a banner, or even a simple branch. Each day of Advent, an ornament is added, representing a key figure or event in salvation history. The ornaments often depict symbols like an apple for Adam and Eve, a rainbow for Noah, a ram for Abraham, a ladder for Jacob, and the Ten Commandments for Moses. Prophets such as Isaiah and Elijah are represented with scrolls or fire, while King David's ornament may feature a crown or harp. The lineage culminates in the greatest gift—Jesus—often symbolized by a manger, a star, or the Chi-Rho.

JESSE TREE COOKIES

THE JESSE TREE IS A BELOVED way to journey through salvation history during Advent. And what better way to bring this tradition to life than through baking? These Jesse Tree cookies combine faith and family, offering a delicious way to reflect on the stories that lead to Christ's birth. Each cookie is shaped or decorated with symbols from Scripture—an apple for Adam and Eve, a star for Abraham, a crown for David. As you bake and decorate together, take time to read the corresponding Scripture passages, deepening your anticipation for the coming of our Savior on Christmas Day.

1. Preheat the oven to 350 degrees F. Lightly grease a baking sheet and set aside.

2. Blend together the butter, brown sugar, egg, almond extract, and salt until smooth. Add the flour and mix thoroughly. Stir in the oats.

3. Chill the dough in the refrigerator for at least 30 minutes and up to 24 hours.

4. Roll out the dough to ⅛-inch thick on a floured surface. Cut into shapes. (Please see the Jesse Tree cookie templates in Appendix I.) Put on the baking sheet.

5. Bake for 8 to 10 minutes until the edges are just set and slightly golden. Remove from the oven and cool.

6. Decorate with icing as desired.

TO MAKE THE ICING:

Mix the confectioners' sugar, meringue powder, vanilla extract, almond extract, corn syrup, and water on high for 3 minutes, adding water by the teaspoon as needed.

INGREDIENTS

YIELDS ABOUT 30 COOKIES

1 cup **butter**, softened

⅔ cup **brown sugar**

1 **egg**

1 teaspoon **almond extract**

½ teaspoon **salt**

2 ½ cups all-purpose **flour**

1 cup **oats**

1 clean coin, such as a quarter, wrapped in silver or gold foil

ROYAL ICING

2 pounds **confectioners' sugar**

⅓ cup **meringue powder**

1 teaspoon **vanilla extract**

1 teaspoon **almond extract**

1 tablespoon **corn syrup**

½ cup **water**

O ANTIPHONS

As Advent draws to a close and the world waits on tiptoe for the birth of Christ, the Church lifts her voice in a series of ancient and poetic prayers known as the O Antiphons. Chanted or recited during Vespers from December 17 to 23, these seven antiphons are a rich spiritual treasury, echoing with the longings of Israel and the deep desires of the human heart.

Each O Antiphon begins with a prophetic title for the coming Messiah—O Wisdom, O Key of David, O Emmanuel—drawn from the Old Testament, especially the Book of Isaiah. These titles reveal the many facets of Jesus' mission: He is the Light for those in darkness, the Deliverer of captives, the King of nations, the Desire of every heart. Each prayer ends with a plea: Come. Come and teach, come and save, come and set us free.

Though their origins stretch back over a thousand years, the O Antiphons remain deeply relevant today. They remind us that Advent is not a passive waiting, but a season of active longing, of hearts crying out for the Savior to come not only to the world, but into our own lives.

FRYING PAN COOKIES

"We knew it was Advent when Mom would start making these cookies. She told us they were to help us prepare for the sweetness of the Christmas season," remembered Sandy Hanson, writer of this recipe.

1. Mix the first three ingredients in a frying pan over medium heat and stir until thick and congealed.

2. Remove from the heat and mix in remaining ingredients except the coconut. Cool the mixture.

3. To help shape the dough, rub some butter on your hands. Shape the dough into small 1-inch balls. Roll each ball in the shredded coconut.

INGREDIENTS

YIELDS 4 DOZEN COOKIES

1 ½ cups **pitted dates**, diced

1 cup **granulated sugar**

2 large **eggs**, slightly beaten

2 ¼ cups **crisped rice cereal**

¼ teaspoon **salt**, to taste (optional)

1 teaspoon **vanilla extract**

About 1 cup **shredded coconut**

Butter for hands

ADVENT CAROLS

In stores and on the radio, "Jingle Bells" and "Joy to the World" begin playing before Thanksgiving has even passed. But within the Church's calendar, Advent and Christmas are distinct seasons, each with its own tone, prayers, and music.

Advent carols are songs of longing, anticipation, and hope. They echo the voices of the prophets and the cry of the human heart awaiting the Savior. These hymns do not yet celebrate Christ's birth, but prepare the soul to receive Him. Their melodies tend to be meditative, their lyrics rich with biblical imagery.

Christmas carols, on the other hand, are joyful proclamations of the Incarnation. Sung from Christmas Day through the Baptism of the Lord, these songs rejoice in the mystery of Emmanuel, God with us. Just as you wouldn't light birthday candles before the guest of honor arrives, the Church waits to sing "Silent Night" until Christ is born.

RED-GREEN SALAD

THIS COLORFUL SALAD HERALDS THE COMING of the Christmas season. Select your own salad dressing, but a classic vinaigrette would be a good choice. Feel free to make substitutions or omit ingredients, if you like—as long as it doesn't compromise the color palette!

1. Put the spinach, grapes, grape tomatoes, red and green peppers, green peas, and pistachio nuts in a large salad bowl. Season with the salt and pepper and toss with the chosen salad dressing.

2. To make a classic vinaigrette, in a small bowl combine vinegar, Dijon mustard, garlic, honey, and salt and pepper to taste. Slowly drizzle in the olive oil, whisking constantly in order to form an emulsion. Alternatively, add the ingredients to a mason jar, affix the lid, and shake vigorously.

3. Garnish with the dried cranberries and chopped fresh parsley.

CLASSIC VINAIGRETTE INGREDIENTS

3 tablespoons **extra virgin olive oil**

1 tablespoon **vinegar** (red, white wine, or apple cider vinegar all work well)

1 teaspoon **Dijon mustard**

1 clove **garlic**, minced

½ teaspoon **honey** or **maple syrup**

Salt and freshly ground **black pepper**, to taste

SALAD INGREDIENTS

SERVES 4 TO 6

2 cups **baby spinach**

1 cup **red seedless grapes**, rinsed

1 cup **green seedless grapes**, rinsed

1 cup **grape tomatoes**, or more as desired

1 large **red bell pepper**, seeded and diced

1 large **green bell pepper**, seeded and diced

1 cup cooked **green peas**

½ cup shelled **pistachio nuts**

Salt and freshly ground **black pepper**, to taste

Salad dressing, to taste (see left)

⅓ cup **dried cranberries**, for garnish

¼ cup chopped **fresh parsley**, for garnish

NOVEMBER 30

ST. ANDREW
THE APOSTLE

— Israel —

Born: circa 5, Died: circa 60

Born in Bethsaida on the Sea of Galilee, St. Andrew was the older brother of St. Peter and a humble fisherman. A disciple of St. John the Baptist, he immediately recognized Jesus as the "Lamb of God" and answered His call to become a "fisher of men" (Matt. 4:18–20; Mark 1:16–18).

Andrew's deep devotion led him to witness Christ's miracles and teachings, even joining Him on the Mount of Olives. After Christ's Ascension, he spread the gospel across Asia Minor, the Black Sea, and Greece. In Patras, he was martyred around A.D. 60, crucified on a diagonal cross, embracing suffering in imitation of his Lord.

St. Andrew's legacy endures as the patron saint of fishermen and numerous nations, including Scotland and Russia. His unwavering faith and evangelization continue to inspire Catholics worldwide. St. Andrew, pray for us!

SCOTTISH COLLOPS

Traditionally served on St. Andrew's Day, the feast day of Scotland's patron saint, Scottish Collops are a hearty, rustic dish that reflects the simplicity and warmth of Scottish cooking. These tender pan-fried slices of beef (or venison) were a popular way to celebrate festive occasions, particularly in the colder months. In honor of St. Andrew, this dish brings a taste of Scotland's culinary heritage to the table.

1. Melt the butter and add 2 tablespoons of olive oil in a large skillet, then add the onions and garlic and sauté until translucent or golden, about 10 minutes. Add the red wine and let simmer to reduce, about 20 minutes.

2. In the meantime, wash and pat dry the steak slices. Season with salt and pepper.

3. In a separate skillet, heat the remaining olive oil, add the steaks, and sauté for up to 3 minutes each side, until browned and cooked to your desired doneness.

4. Remove the steaks to a plate and cover with foil. (They will continue to cook.)

5. Add the Worcestershire sauce, cumin, coriander, and turmeric to the pan. Cook for up to 3 minutes, until they form a paste, then pour into the wine and onion glaze and stir well. Top the steaks with the glaze and serve.

INGREDIENTS

SERVES 4 TO 6

4 tablespoons **butter**

4 tablespoon **olive oil**

3 to 4 medium **onions**, peeled and sliced

4 cloves **garlic**, peeled and minced

1 cup **red wine**

8 thin (⅜-inch thick) slices of **rump steak**

Salt and freshly ground **black pepper**, to taste

1 tablespoon **Worcestershire sauce**

1 teaspoon ground **cumin**

1 teaspoon ground **coriander**

1 teaspoon ground **turmeric**

Side dishes for this entrée could include puréed sweet potatoes and steamed brussels sprouts.

DECEMBER 4

ST. BARBARA

— Nicomedia —

Born: Mid-third century,
Died: Late-third century

Born in the mid-third century, St. Barbara was the daughter of a wealthy pagan named Dioscorus. Fearing the outside world's influence, he confined her to a tower, allowing only pagan teachers to visit. Yet, as she gazed upon the beauty of creation, she recognized the hand of the true Creator. It was this Creator to whom Barbara dedicated her life while still in captivity.

When her father eventually freed her, hoping she would accept marriage, Barbara instead sought out fellow Christians, deepening her faith. She received Baptism from a priest disguised as a merchant. Upon learning of her conversion, her father was enraged. She fled, but he captured her, beat her, and turned her over to the authorities. Despite brutal torture, she refused to renounce Christ. Her father ultimately beheaded her, but divine justice prevailed—he was struck down by lightning.

St. Barbara is honored as one of the Fourteen Holy Helpers. May her intercession strengthen us in trials, as we, too, seek the light of Christ.

ST. BARBARA'S BREAD

Sᴛ. Bᴀʀʙᴀʀᴀ'ꜱ ꜰᴇᴀꜱᴛ ᴅᴀʏ ꜰᴇᴀᴛᴜʀᴇꜱ ᴛʀᴀᴅɪᴛɪᴏɴᴀʟ breads and other wheat foods symbolizing the harvest, with overtones of death and rebirth, tying her feast day to Christmas. In France and Ukraine, two or more grains of wheat are planted and forced to grow. Folklore states that if they flourish by Christmas Eve, the wheat crop will prosper that year.

1. Dissolve the yeast in warm water. Set aside for 5 minutes. Meanwhile, heat the milk, sugar, butter, and salt until warm (105 to 115 degrees F).

2. Combine the yeast mixture, milk mixture, egg, lemon juice, nutmeg, allspice, and cinnamon. Add 1 cup flour and slivered almonds. Mix thoroughly. Add enough remaining flour to make a soft dough. Knead on lightly floured surface until smooth, about 10 minutes. Place the dough in a greased bowl, turning to coat top.

3. Cover; let rise in warm place until doubled, about 1 hour.

4. Preheat the oven to 350 degrees F. Punch down the dough. Divide into thirds. Roll each third into a rope, approximately 10 to 12 inches long. Lay the dough portions side by side on a lightly floured work surface. Pinch the tips together so they are attached on one end. Take the right rope and cross it over the middle rope (it will become the new middle). Take the left rope and cross it over the new middle rope. Repeat: right over middle, left over middle, alternating until you reach the end. Once you reach the end, pinch the ends together and tuck underneath the loaf. Place the loaf on a greased baking sheet. Let rise in a warm place until almost doubled in size, about 30 minutes.

5. Bake for 35 to 40 minutes, or until done. Cool on a wire rack. Frost with Confectioners' Icing. If desired, decorate with almonds.

TO MAKE THE ICING:

Mix ingredients thoroughly. With spoon, drizzle icing back and forth across the loaf. If desired, add nuts or fruits as decorations before icing sets.

DOUGH INGREDIENTS

SERVES 4 TO 6

¼ cup **milk**

¼ cup **granulated sugar**

2 tablespoons **unsalted butter**

¼ teaspoon **salt**

1 ½ teaspoons **active dry yeast**

2 tablespoons **warm water** (105 to 115 degrees F)

1 **egg**

½ tablespoon **lemon juice**

½ teaspoon grated **nutmeg**

½ teaspoon ground **allspice**

½ teaspoon ground **cinnamon**

1 to 1 ½ cups **all-purpose flour**

⅓ cup **slivered almonds**

Confectioners' Icing (see below)

Whole almonds, if desired

CONFECTIONERS' ICING

½ cup **confectioners' sugar**

½ teaspoon **vanilla extract**

1 to 2 tablespoons **milk**

DECEMBER 6

ST. NICHOLAS

— Myra —

Born: 270, Died: 343

Born in A.D. 270 in Asia Minor, St. Nicholas was raised in a devout Christian home and mentored by his uncle, the bishop of Patara, who ordained him a priest. Chosen as bishop of Myra, Nicholas endured persecution, imprisonment, and torture for his faith until Emperor Constantine freed him.

A fierce defender of orthodoxy, St. Nicholas fought against paganism and heresies like Arianism, even toppling temples dedicated to false gods. Legends tell of his miraculous deeds, including calming a storm at sea, making him the patron saint of sailors and travelers. Yet he is best known for his boundless generosity. A well-known legend of St. Nicholas tells of how he delivered bags of gold to a poor man in the middle of the night. These little bags of gold were a dowry for the poor man's daughters, enabling the girls to marry. Without a dowry for marriage, the girls would have lived a life of servitude.

St. Nicholas died in A.D. 343, and his relics, enshrined in Myra, became a pilgrimage site. He is the patron saint of sailors, merchants, children, and countless others, venerated across Europe and beyond. His feast day, December 6, reminds us of his selfless charity and steadfast faith—calling us to give generously and defend truth in our own lives.

BAKLAVA SATCHELS

INSPIRED BY THE GENEROSITY OF ST. Nicholas, this recipe is a sweet nod to the saint's legendary gift-giving spirit. These flaky pastry pouches, filled with spiced nuts, symbolize the small bags of gold he famously left for those in need. Perfect for celebrating his feast day, they blend Old World flavors with a sense of festive wonder.

1. Preheat the oven to 375 degrees F.

2. In a medium bowl, stir together chopped nuts, melted butter, honey, orange, cinnamon, and salt until evenly combined.

3. Stack the thawed phyllo sheets on top of each other. Using a sharp knife, cut the sheets lengthwise in half and cut each length crosswise into thirds, to make 6 sections per sheet of phyllo. Cover phyllo with a barely damp kitchen towel to prevent from drying.

4. Prepare a clean work surface and set the melted butter and pastry brush within easy reach before you start assembling. Place one square of phyllo on the work surface. Brush lightly with melted butter. Top with a second square of phyllo, offsetting the corners. Brush lightly with melted butter. Top with a third square of phyllo, offsetting the corners again to form a star shape. Brush with butter.

5. Place two tablespoons of filling in the center of the phyllo. Enclose by bringing together two opposite sides. Continue to gather the edges while twisting and pleating them slightly to form a pouch. Brush the top and sides lightly with melted butter.

6. Place on a baking sheet (leave an inch or two of space around each one) and bake until tops are golden brown, about 18 to 25 minutes. Remove from the oven and place the baking sheet on a rack to cool for 5 to 10 minutes. Serve warm.

INGREDIENTS

YIELDS 12 TO 13 SATCHELS

FILLING

1 ½ cups **mixed nuts**, such as pistachios, walnuts, and pecans, lightly toasted and chopped

1 tablespoon **unsalted butter**, melted

¼ cup **honey**, plus more for serving

Zest from ¼ **orange**

¼ teaspoon ground **cinnamon**

Pinch **salt**

PASTRY

1 package (9 x 13 inches) frozen **phyllo pastry sheets**, thawed

¼ cup **unsalted butter**, melted

Let Us Pray

Thou art all fair, O Mary! And the original stain is not in thee! Thou art the glory of Jerusalem! Thou, the joy of Israel! Thou art the honor of our people! Thou art the advocate of sinners! O Mary! Virgin most prudent! Mother most merciful! Pray for us, intercede for us with Our Lord Jesus Christ. Amen.

SOLEMNITY OF THE IMMACULATE CONCEPTION

— Holy Day of Obligation —

DECEMBER 8

The Feast of the Immaculate Conception, celebrated on December 8, honors the Virgin Mary's pure and sinless beginning in her mother's womb. This solemnity, a Holy Day of Obligation in the United States and many other countries, prepares our hearts for the birth of Christ by recognizing Mary's unique role in salvation history.

Chosen to be the mother of the Savior, Mary was granted the singular privilege of being conceived without original sin. The angel Gabriel's greeting at the Annunciation—"full of grace" (Luke 1:28)—confirms this divine gift. As proclaimed by Pope Pius IX in the 1854 Apostolic Constitution *Ineffabilis Deus*, "The most Blessed Virgin Mary, in the first instance of her conception, by a singular grace and privilege granted by Almighty God, in view of the merits of Jesus Christ, the Savior of the human race, was preserved free from all stain of original sin."

This great mystery reminds us that God's grace works beyond time, preparing Mary to give her perfect "yes" to His plan. As we celebrate this feast, we honor the purity and faith of Our Lady, seeking her intercession that we, too, may open our hearts fully to God's will.

THREE-CHEESE CHICKEN ALFREDO BAKE

ACCORDING TO COOK KENDRA TIERNEY, "THREE-CHEESE Chicken Alfredo Bake is cheesy heaven with the ricotta, parmesan and mozzarella cheeses. Each bite is creamy and delicious." But what makes this dish a perfect fit for celebrating the Feast of the Immaculate Conception? The alfredo bake casserole is all white, representing Mary's purity.

1. Preheat the oven to 375 degrees F. Grease a 9-inch x 13-inch baking dish and set aside.

2. Bring a large pot of water to a boil and cook the pasta al dente, according to the package instructions. Drain the pasta, reserving ½ cup of water, and return the pasta to the pot.

3. Meanwhile, make the alfredo sauce by melting the butter in a medium saucepan over medium heat. Add 3 cloves of minced garlic and sauté for about 30 seconds until fragrant. Pour in the heavy cream and simmer for 2 to 3 minutes, stirring frequently. Reduce the heat to low and slowly add the parmesan cheese, stirring continuously until it melts and the sauce is smooth. Season with salt and pepper and nutmeg, if desired. Lastly, add in ½ cup of pasta water and stir to combine.

4. Add the alfredo sauce, chicken, ricotta cheese, sour cream, parmesan cheese, garlic, Italian seasoning, and parsley to the cooked pasta. Stir together to combine.

5. Pour the mixture into the baking dish, spreading out evenly. Sprinkle the top evenly with mozzarella cheese.

6. Bake, uncovered, for 30 minutes, or until hot and bubbly. Serve warm and enjoy!

INGREDIENTS

SERVES 6 TO 8

12 to 16 ounces **penne pasta**

Alfredo sauce (see note)

2 cups cooked chopped **chicken**

One 15-ounce container **ricotta cheese**

1 cup **sour cream**

¼ cup grated **parmesan cheese**

2 cloves **garlic**, peeled and minced

1 tablespoon **Italian seasoning**, or more as desired

2 teaspoons chopped dried **parsley**

2 cups shredded **mozzarella cheese**

ALFREDO SAUCE

6 tablespoons **butter**

3 cloves **garlic**, minced

1 ½ cups **heavy cream**

1 ½ cups **parmesan cheese**, grated

Salt and **pepper**, to taste

¼ teaspoon **nutmeg** (optional)

½ cup **pasta water**

Instead of making your own alfredo sauce, you can use 1 ½ 15-ounce bottles of store-bought alfredo sauce.

DECEMBER 12

OUR LADY OF GUADALUPE

— Tepeyac Hill —

On December 9, 1531, a humble peasant, Juan Diego, was on his way to Mass when the Blessed Virgin Mary appeared to him on Tepeyac Hill in Mexico. Radiant like the sun and carrying the Child Jesus, she asked him to tell the bishop to build a chapel on the hill. When Juan Diego shared this with the bishop, the bishop hesitated, requesting a sign.

In a later apparition, Our Lady comforted Juan Diego and instructed him to gather flowers from the frozen hilltop. Miraculously, he found roses blooming in winter and placed them in his tilma. When he opened his cloak before the bishop, the breathtaking image of Our Lady of Guadalupe was imprinted on the fabric — a heavenly confirmation of her request.

Awestruck, the bishop ordered the chapel's construction. Devotion to Our Lady of Guadalupe spread rapidly.

Today, Our Lady of Guadalupe is the beloved patron of the Americas, the unborn, and countless dioceses worldwide. Her feast day, December 12, is joyfully celebrated with Masses, processions, and festive meals — reminders of her tender love and unfailing protection.

CHICKEN MOLE

A TRUE MOLE MAY TAKE HOURS or days to prepare properly because numerous spices, dried chiles, nuts, seeds, and garlic are ground together to produce the beloved ingredient in so many Mexican recipes. Its origins are unclear, though one theory suggests it was invented by a nun in Puebla to honor an archbishop, while another claims it dates back to when Montezuma ruled over Aztec Mexico. This chicken *mole* recipe actually compiles its own version of mole using Mexican chocolate, *pasilla* chiles, garlic, and spices. Serve this with a side of cooked rice.

1. Soak the pasilla chiles in ½ cup water for 20 minutes. Drain and discard the water.

2. In a large skillet, add the olive oil, chopped onions, and chopped garlic. Cook for 5 to 10 minutes over medium heat until the onions become transparent. Add the chiles, chicken broth, Mexican chocolate, peanut butter, and fresh oregano, and continue cooking until well combined.

3. Put the ingredients into a blender or food processor. Add the chopped tostadas and sugar and blend until well combined.

4. Add the sauce to a saucepan and bring to a boil. Reduce the heat to low and cook for 20 minutes, stirring occasionally. Add the salt and pepper to taste.

5. Slice the cooked chicken into cubes or long, flat strips. Add the chicken to the mole sauce and serve on plates with cooked rice on the side. Sprinkle each serving with sesame seeds.

A quick note on Mexican chocolate—Mexican chocolate is a rich, slightly gritty chocolate made from roasted cacao, sugar, and cinnamon, often used in traditional drinks and desserts. You should be able to find it in the Mexican food aisle of your local grocery store.

INGREDIENTS

SERVES 4 TO 6

5 **pasilla chiles**, stemmed and seeded

4 tablespoons **olive oil**

2 cups chopped **onions**

4 cloves **garlic**, peeled and chopped

2 ½ to 3 cups **chicken broth**

5 ½ to 6 ½ ounces **Mexican chocolate**, chopped (see note)

4 tablespoons smooth **peanut butter**

1 teaspoon chopped fresh **oregano**

3 **corn tostadas**, torn into pieces

1 ½ tablespoons **granulated sugar**

Salt and freshly ground **black pepper**, to taste

3 boneless **chicken breasts**, baked

3 boneless **chicken thighs**, baked

Sesame seeds, for garnish

DECEMBER 13

ST. LUCY

Born: 283, Died: 304

Born in A.D. 283 in Syracuse, Sicily, St. Lucy was raised in a noble Roman family. After her mother was miraculously healed through the intercession of St. Agatha, Lucy secretly vowed her life to God, committing herself to chastity and charity.

When her mother arranged a marriage to a pagan suitor, Lucy refused, declaring her devotion to Christ. Enraged, the rejected suitor betrayed her as a Christian to the governor, Paschasius, who sought to force her into a brothel. By God's power, Lucy remained immovable and attempts to burn her alive failed. She was ultimately executed by the sword.

A legend recounts that her eyes were removed before death, but when her body was prepared for burial, they were miraculously restored. Her relics were venerated in Sicily and later transferred to Italy, spreading devotion to her courage and purity.

St. Lucy, whose name means "light," is the patroness of the blind, those with eye disorders, and the poor. Honored on December 13, her feast is celebrated with candles and special foods, reminding us that Christ's light shines even in the darkest trials. May her witness inspire us to stand firm in faith.

ST. LUCIA BUNS

TRADITIONALLY, ST. LUCY'S FEAST DAY WAS a celebration of lights. On early calendars the day would fall on the winter solstice, the shortest and darkest day of the year. Families can celebrate the day by waking up early and enjoying a sweet breakfast, hanging Christmas lights, having children dress up as St. Lucy, and honoring the saint with songs and prayers.

1. In a small saucepan set over medium heat (or in a micro-wave-safe bowl in the microwave), heat the milk and saffron to a simmer; remove from the heat and stir in the butter. Allow the mixture to cool to room temperature, about 30 to 35 minutes. You can reduce the milk's cooling time by about 10 minutes by refrigerating it.

2. Weigh your flour or measure it by gently spooning it into a cup, then leveling off any excess. In a large bowl or the bowl of a stand mixer, whisk together the yeast, flours, salt, and sugar.

3. To the milk mixture, whisk in the 2 whole eggs, 1 egg yolk, and vanilla extract. Pour the mixture over the top of the dry ingredients. Mix to combine, then knead for about 7 minutes by mixer, about 10 minutes by hand, until the dough is smooth and supple. Place the dough in a lightly greased bowl, cover it, and let it rise for 1 hour, or until it's quite puffy, though not necessarily doubled in size.

4. Gently deflate the dough and divide it into 12 equal pieces. If you have a scale, each piece will weigh 3 ¼ ounces. Shape the pieces of dough into rough logs and let them rest, covered, for about 10 minutes.

INGREDIENTS

YIELD: 12 LARGE BUNS

BUNS

1 cup **milk**

¼ teaspoon lightly crushed **saffron threads**

8 tablespoons **unsalted butter**, at room temperature

4 ½ cups **unbleached all-purpose flour**

1 tablespoon **instant yeast**

¼ cup **potato flour** or ½ cup **dried potato flakes** (instant mashed potatoes)

1 ½ teaspoons **salt** (Reduce to 1 ¼ teaspoons if you use salted butter)

⅓ cup **granulated sugar**

2 large **eggs**

1 large **egg**, separated

1 teaspoon **vanilla extract**

5. Roll each log into a 15-inch to 18-inch rope. It's okay if they shrink after you stop rolling them. Shape each rope into an "S" shape. Tuck a golden raisin into the center of each of the coils. Place the buns on a lightly greased or parchment-lined baking sheet, leaving an inch or so between them. Cover them, and let them rise for about 30 minutes, till they're noticeably puffy, but not doubled in size. While they're rising, preheat the oven to 375 degrees F. Brush each bun with some of the egg white mixture. Sprinkle with coarse white Swedish pearl sugar.

6. Bake the buns until they're golden brown, about 18 to 20 minutes. If you've used raisins, tent them with foil for the final 3 minutes to prevent the raisins from burning. Remove the buns from the oven and transfer them to a rack to cool.

TOPPING

1 large **egg white** (reserved from dough) mixed with 1 tablespoon **cold water**

Swedish pearl sugar (optional) (see note)

Golden raisins (optional)

Pearl sugar is a popular European ingredient that adds crunch to baked goods.

CHRISTMAS SEASON

Let Us Pray

Let the just rejoice, for their Justifier is born. Let the sick and infirm rejoice, for their Savior is born. Let the captives rejoice, for their Redeemer is born. Let slaves rejoice, for their Master is born. Let free men rejoice, for their Liberator is born. Let All Christians rejoice, for Jesus Christ is born. —St. Augustine of Hippo

CHRISTMAS SEASON

The world waits in hushed anticipation during Advent, but when Christmas arrives, the heavens burst forth in song—for Christ the Savior is born! The Christmas season is a time of profound joy, celebrating the mystery of the Incarnation, when God Himself took on human flesh to dwell among us. With the birth of Jesus in Bethlehem, the world was forever changed. The long-awaited Messiah, foretold by the prophets, came in humility, wrapped in swaddling clothes and laid in a manger, yet He is the King of Kings, the Light that darkness cannot overcome.

For Catholics, Christmas is more than a single day—it is a sacred season, beginning on December 25 and extending through the Feast of the Baptism of the Lord (also known as Candlemas). Throughout these holy days, the Church rejoices in the birth of Christ and reflects on the unfolding mystery of our salvation. The feasts of St. Stephen, the Holy Family, Mary, the Mother of God, and the Epiphany remind us that Christmas is not just about looking back to Bethlehem, but about welcoming Christ into our hearts each day.

This season is one of faith, family, and festivity, as we gather to celebrate the greatest gift ever given—Emmanuel, "God with us" (Matt. 1:23). As we share meals with loved ones, may our feasting reflect the joy of the heavenly banquet to come. Let us open our hearts to Christ's peace, remembering that the true gift of Christmas is the love of God made visible in Jesus, our Redeemer and King.

> *The Christmas season's liturgical color is white, which represents light, purity, and joy, or gold, which represents joy. While we can festively celebrate with the season's red and green, let us not forget to add white and gold to our table to commemorate these glorious liturgical colors.*

CHRISTMAS DAY FEAST

Homemade Eggnog

Sweet-Savory Fish Soup

Easy Baked Ham with
Maple and Brown Sugar Glaze

Mashed Sweet Potatoes

Green Beans with Pistachios and Raisins

Christmas Dinner Rolls with
Brown Butter and Rosemary

Gaudete Mincemeat Pies

Crispy Ginger Cookies

Let Us Pray

"And you, Mary, the *Virgin of expectation and fulfilment*, who hold the secret of Christmas, make us able to recognize in the Child whom you hold in your arms the heralded Saviour, who brings hope and peace to all. With you we worship him and trustingly say: we need You, Redeemer of man, You who know the hopes and fears of our hearts. Come and stay with us, Lord! May the joy of your Nativity reach to the farthest ends of the universe!" — Pope St. John Paul II

THE NATIVITY OF THE LORD

CHRISTMAS

DECEMBER 25

Christmas, the Solemnity of the Nativity of Our Lord, celebrates the moment that changed history: "God became man to make us children of God," as St. Irenaeus wrote. The true joy of Christmas is found in the angel's proclamation: "For to you is born this day in the city of David a Savior, who is Christ the Lord" (Luke 2:11).

Though the Gospels do not record the exact date of Christ's birth, December 25 first appeared in a Roman calendar in the third century. Some scholars suggest this date was chosen to counter pagan festivals, while others point to its connection with March 25, traditionally observed as the Annunciation—placing Christ's birth exactly nine months later.

By the Middle Ages, Christmas had become a grand celebration, marked by noble feasts. King Richard II of England famously hosted a banquet featuring twelve oxen and three hundred sheep. Meanwhile, Christian traditions flourished. The Christmas tree, a beloved symbol, originated with German Christians who decorated evergreens with fruits and gingerbread. Another enduring figure, Santa Claus, traces his roots to St. Nicholas of Myra, a generous bishop known for his care of the poor and children. Dutch immigrants later brought "Sinterklaas" to America, shaping the modern Santa Claus.

As we gather to celebrate Christ's birth, may our feasting reflect the deep joy of the Incarnation—God's great gift of love to the world.

SHOPPING LIST

ALCOHOL

Dark or spiced rum, bourbon, or brandy	1 ¼ cup
White wine	⅓ cup

BAKING SUPPLIES

All-purpose flour	4 cups
Baking soda	
Bread flour	2 ½ cups
Confectioners' sugar	
Instant dry yeast	2 teaspoons
Light brown sugar	3 ½ cups
Molasses, unsulphured	⅓ cup
Sea salt	
Shortening	2 tablespoons
Sugar, granulated	2 cups

CANNED GOODS

Crispy fried onions	1 cup
Pineapple juice	½ cup
Pineapple slices (fresh or canned)	
Vegetable broth	2 cups

CONDIMENTS AND SAUCES

Dijon mustard	¼ cup
Maple syrup	¾ cup

DRY FOODS

Dried apricots	½ cup
Dried cherries	½ cup
Dried cranberries	½ cup
Pistachios, shelled	½ cup
Raisins	2 cups
Walnuts (or almonds)	

EGGS AND DAIRY

Butter, unsalted	7 sticks
Eggs	1 dozen large
Heavy Cream	4 cups
Milk	2 ¼ cups

MEAT

Ham, pre-cooked and non-spiral cut	8–10 pound ham
Seafood (firm white fish, shrimp, scallops, and/or crabmeat)	1 pound

OIL AND VINEGAR

Apple cider vinegar	3 tablespoons
Olive oil	

PRODUCE

Apples	2 large
Carrots	3 medium
Dill	1 small bunch
Garlic	1 head
Green beans	1 ½ pounds
Kohlrabi	1 large
Lemon	2 large
Onion, white	2 large
Orange	1 large
Parsley	1 bunch
Roasted red pepper	
Rosemary	
Scallions	1 bunch
Sweet potatoes	4 pounds

SPICES

Allspice, ground	Ginger, ground
Cinnamon, ground	Nutmeg, ground
Cloves, ground	Vanilla extract
Cloves, whole	White pepper, ground
Coriander, ground	

HOMEMADE EGGNOG

According to some historians, eggnog was first imbibed as far back as the thirteenth century by medieval monks in Britain. What they sipped was an ale with eggs and figs. By the seventeenth century, sherry became an important ingredient, and nobility used this beverage to toast someone's health. Then American colonists switched out sherry and other European liquors and added Caribbean rum instead. Eventually, eggnog—with or without an alcoholic addition—became a holiday favorite beverage throughout the country.

1. In a medium-sized bowl, whisk together the egg yolks with the sugar until creamy, about 3 minutes. In a medium-sized saucepan, combine the cream, milk, cloves, nutmeg, and salt. Heat over medium-high heat, stirring often until the mixture simmers. Do not boil!

2. Using a large ladle, slowly transfer a spoonful of the hot milk mixture into the bowl with the creamed egg mixture, whisking rapidly until smooth. Repeat until the milk mixture is used up. Pour back into the saucepan and heat over medium-high heat, whisking constantly for about 3 minutes or until slightly thickened. Do not boil. It will thicken more as it cools.

3. Remove from the heat and add the vanilla and cinnamon. Strain the mixture into a pitcher, cover, and let cool. Refrigerate until chilled. Serve with whipped cream and nutmeg and cinnamon dusted on top. Optionally, add about ¼ cup of dark or spiced rum, bourbon, or brandy to each glass before serving.

INGREDIENTS

SERVES 4

6 large **egg yolks**

½ cup **granulated sugar**

2 cups **heavy cream** and 1 cup **milk** (recommended), or 1 ½ cups of each

4 whole **cloves**

½ teaspoon ground **nutmeg**, plus extra for dusting

Pinch **salt**

½ teaspoon **vanilla extract**

½ teaspoon ground **cinnamon**

1 cup dark or **spiced rum**, **bourbon**, or **brandy** (optional)

For Toppings:

whipped cream, dash of **nutmeg**, dash of **cinnamon**

SWEET-SAVORY FISH SOUP

According to some sources, the Greek word *ichthys*, meaning "Jesus Christ, Son of God, Savior," also means "the Jesus fish." As the Gospels note, Jesus fed about five thousand people with some bread and two fish. How fitting, then, to launch a festive Christmas dinner with a bowl of savory fish soup?

According to the recipe donor, "Preparation takes about 90 minutes, from grating vegetables to deveining shrimp. If you wish to serve it with a white wine, a Chardonnay is a full-bodied choice. To add a bit of spiciness, add a drizzle of hot sauce or a sprinkling of minced red pepper. If you're making the soup the day before, add the last step after reheating it the following day."

1. Mix the mirepoix of carrots, onions, scallions, and garlic in a large mixing bowl. Next, in a large skillet over medium-high heat, melt the stick of butter without letting it brown. Once melted, add the mirepoix mixture and sauté until the onions become translucent, about 7 to 10 minutes. Add the broth and the white wine or sherry, letting the mixture simmer for about 10 minutes.

2. Move this mixture to a large stockpot, add the kohlrabi and sweet potatoes, and simmer over low heat for about 15 minutes. (If you care for a stronger seafood taste, you could add at this point some fish fumet paste, lobster paste, or clam juice.)

3. Wash and dab dry the fish fillet and peel and devein the shrimp. Melt 2 tablespoons of butter in a medium-sized skillet over medium heat. Add the seafood, flip over after 4 minutes, and cook for 2 to 3 minutes more. They still should be slightly translucent (they'll fully cook in the soup later).

INGREDIENTS

SERVES 4 TO 6

MIREPOIX

2 cups shredded **carrot**

2 cups chopped **onions**

1 bunch **scallions**, finely sliced (or 4 stalks **celery** or a medium **fennel bulb**, diced)

4 cloves **garlic**, peeled and minced

8 tablespoons **unsalted butter**

2 cups **vegetable broth** or one cup each of **vegetable** and/or **chicken** and/or **fish broth**, or more as needed

⅓ cup of **white wine** or **sherry**

4. While the seafood is cooking, scoop half of the cooled vegetable mix into a separate bowl, pot, or blender, and purée with a wand or in the blender. Add the heavy cream and purée until smooth. Add the egg yolks and purée until smooth. Transfer this mixture back to the stock pot.

5. Remove the skin from the fish and discard. Flake fish with a fork into bite-sized pieces. Cut shrimp up into bite-sized pieces. (Do the same with other seafood you might have selected.) Add the seafood to the stockpot. Reheat, but do not boil. Season with ground white pepper, salt if needed, lemon juice and lemon zest to taste, or another splash of white wine. Before serving, sprinkle with chopped fresh dill and garnish (optional) with a slice of roasted red pepper.

SOUP

2 cups shredded **kohlrabi** or similar vegetable, such as turnip or other root vegetable

2 cups shredded **sweet potato** or something similar, such as regular potato or other root vegetable

2 tablespoons **unsalted butter**

About 1 pound **seafood**, including a firm white fish fillet, some shrimp, scallops, and/or crabmeat

2 cups **heavy cream**

2 **egg yolks**

Ground **white pepper**, to taste

Salt, to taste

Lemon juice and **lemon zest**, to taste (optional)

Fresh **dill**, chopped, to taste and for garnish

A piece of **roasted red pepper**, for garnish (optional)

EASY BAKED HAM WITH MAPLE AND BROWN SUGAR GLAZE

Celebrate the joy of Christmas Day with a rich and flavorful glazed ham, perfect for gathering family and friends around the table. The sweet glaze caramelizes beautifully, adding a festive touch to this centerpiece dish.

1. Preheat the oven to 325 degrees F. Remove any netting from the ham. Pat the ham dry with paper towels.

2. Score the surface of the ham about ¼-inch deep in a diamond pattern. The lines should be about 1 inch apart. Place the ham, flat side down, in a roasting pan.

3. In a medium-sized saucepan, mix the maple syrup, brown sugar, pineapple juice, Dijon mustard, apple cider vinegar, and ground ginger. Heat over medium heat, stirring until the sugar dissolves and the mixture thickens slightly, about 15 minutes.

4. Brush half the glaze on the ham, making sure it gets into the scores. Arrange the pineapple slices on the ham, if using, and secure them with toothpicks.

5. Cover the ham loosely with foil, and bake, basting with the remaining glaze, every 20 to 30 minutes. Remove the foil for the last 30 minutes.

6. Bake for 10 to 15 minutes per pound, adjusting the time based on your ham's specific cooking instructions. Once the internal temperature reaches 140 degrees F, remove from the oven and let rest 10 minutes before slicing.

INGREDIENTS

SERVES 8 TO 10

8- to 10-pound **precooked ham**, non-spiral cut

¾ cup **maple syrup**

¾ cup **brown sugar**

½ cup **pineapple juice**

¼ cup **Dijon mustard**

1 tablespoon **apple cider vinegar**

1 teaspoon ground **ginger**

Pineapple slices, for garnish (optional)

GREEN BEANS WITH PISTACHIOS AND RAISINS

IT'S UNCLEAR JUST EXACTLY WHAT ANCIENT Israelites ate, but according to this passage from Genesis 43:11, pistachios were a staple. "Then their father Israel said to them, 'If it must be so, then do this: take some of the choice fruits of the land in your bags, and carry down to the man a present, a little balm and a little honey, gum, myrrh, pistachio nuts, and almonds.'" Other favorite foods include raisins and apricots, which add a delightfully sweet touch to this side dish.

1. Place the green beans in a 3-quart saucepan and cover with water. Bring the water to a boil over medium-high heat and blanch the green beans for about 5 minutes. Remove them from the heat, drain off the water, and dry them with a paper towel.

2. Heat the olive oil and butter in a large skillet over medium heat. Add the minced garlic and stir, continuing to cook until the garlic turns golden. Add the raisins, chopped dried apricots, and pistachios. Continue to cook until the nuts turn golden brown. Add the green beans, and stir well, cooking the mixture until the beans are softened.

3. Season the mixture with salt and pepper, to taste. Remove from the skillet and place on a serving platter. Garnish with the onion rings and chopped parsley.

INGREDIENTS

SERVES 6 TO 8

1 ½ pounds **green beans**, washed and trimmed

2 tablespoons **olive oil**

1 tablespoon **butter**, plus more for toasting the pistachios

3 cloves **garlic**, peeled and minced

¾ cup **raisins**, for garnish

½ cup chopped **dried apricots**

½ cup shelled **pistachios**

Salt and freshly ground **black pepper**, to taste

1 cup **crispy fried onions**, for garnish

½ cup chopped **parsley**, for garnish

CHRISTMAS DINNER ROLLS WITH BROWN BUTTER AND ROSEMARY

1. Place a small saucepan on low heat and melt 1/4 cup butter. While stirring occasionally, allow the butter to turn a golden brown color (keep a close eye on it because this goes quickly). Allow the brown butter to cool before adding it to a large bowl or stand mixer.

2. Heat ¾ cup milk in the microwave for 1 minute on HIGH. Add to the bowl along with 2 tablespoons of brown sugar, 1 large egg, 2 teaspoons of chopped fresh rosemary, 1 teaspoon of salt, ½ teaspoon of freshly ground black pepper, 2 ½ cups of bread flour, and 2 teaspoons of instant yeast.

3. Mix the dough on low speed or by hand until all ingredients are moistened, forming a shaggy ball. Using a dough hook, mix on medium-low speed for 5 to 10 minutes, or turn the dough out onto a floured surface and knead until smooth and elastic, 10 to 20 minutes. Place the dough in a lightly greased bowl, cover, and allow the dough to rise in a warm place for 1 to 1 ½ hours, until doubled in size.

4. Preheat the oven to 375 degrees F. Deflate and remove the dough to a floured surface. Divide the dough into 15 equal pieces and form into smooth balls. Arrange on a round pizza pan 13-inches or larger, in a single or double circle. Cover and allow to rise until almost doubled in size. If desired, brush with melted butter and chopped rosemary. Sprinkle lightly with sea salt.

5. Bake for 12 to 15 minutes until golden brown. Remove from the oven and serve.

INGREDIENTS
MAKES 15 ROLLS

¼ cup **butter**

¾ cup **milk**

2 tablespoons **brown sugar**

1 large **egg**

2 teaspoons chopped fresh **rosemary**, plus extra for sprinkling

1 teaspoon **salt**

½ teaspoon freshly ground **black pepper** (optional)

2 ½ cups **bread flour**

2 teaspoons **instant yeast** (see note)

Sea salt, for sprinkling

You can substitute active dry yeast for instant yeast. Dissolving it first is optional. Active dry yeast tends to rise slowly initially but will eventually catch up.

GAUDETE MINCEMEAT PIES

Celebrate the joy of Christ's birth with this festive mincemeat pie, a traditional Christmas treat with roots dating back to medieval England. Originally a spiced meat pie symbolizing the gifts of the Magi, today's sweet version—filled with dried fruits, warm spices, and brandy—honors the rich history of Christmas feasting and the spirit of the season.

1. Put the ingredients for the mincemeat filling in a food processor and chop until the fruits and nuts become a consistent texture. Then simmer the ingredients over medium heat for 15 minutes—this will help the flavors come together. If you are using alcohol, be sure to heat the mixture longer and until almost all the liquid has evaporated, about 25 to 30 minutes.

2. Put the filling in the refrigerator to chill while making the pie crust. Clean out the food processor and add the flour, sugar, and salt. Add the butter and shortening on top. Start processing, pouring some water slowly through the feed tube until the dough starts to form a ball.

3. Preheat the oven to 375 degrees F. Roll two-thirds of the crust out onto a floured surface until ⅛-inch thick. Cut circles out that will fit your muffin tins. Roll out the remaining crust and make stars, lattices, or circle lids to decorate the pie tops.

4. Grease the muffin tins and carefully press the crusts into them, then fill them with the mincemeat mixture. Top each with the additional shapes and lightly brush the top with an egg wash.

5. Bake the pies for 10 to 15 minutes, or until golden brown. Remove them from the oven and carefully remove each from the muffin tins to cool on a wire rack. Sprinkle with confectioners' sugar before serving.

INGREDIENTS

MAKES 12 MINI
PIES OR TARTS

MINCEMEAT FILLING
2 cups chopped **apples** (about
2 apples)

2 cups **brown sugar**

1 ¼ cups **raisins**

½ cup **dried cranberries**

½ cup **dried cherries**

2 tablespoons grated **orange peel**

2 tablespoons grated **lemon peel**

1 ½ tablespoons **walnuts** or **almonds**

Juice of 1 **lemon**

2 tablespoons **apple cider vinegar**

½ cup **unsalted butter**, at room temperature

1 ½ teaspoons ground **cinnamon**

½ teaspoon ground **nutmeg**

¼ teaspoon ground **cloves**

MINCEMEAT FILLING INGREDIENTS CONTINUED

¼ teaspoon ground **ginger**

¼ teaspoon ground **coriander**

¼ teaspoon **salt**

4 tablespoons **rum** or **brandy** (optional)

1 **egg**

Confectioners' sugar, for dusting

PIE CRUST INGREDIENTS

1 ½ cups **all-purpose flour**

1 tablespoon **granulated sugar**

½ teaspoon **salt**

6 tablespoons cold **butter**, cut into pieces

2 tablespoons **shortening**

3 tablespoons **ice water**

CRISPY GINGER COOKIES

According to Jenn Segal who posted this recipe, "They are a treat any time of day (yes, even breakfast), and they fill the house with the most heavenly aroma as they bake. With their deep amber color and slightly crackled tops, they're perfect for the holidays. Think of them as the more delicious cousins of gingerbread men and molasses cookies, offering a rich taste and a delightful texture that traditional holiday cut-out cookies just can't match."

1. In a medium bowl, whisk together the flour, baking soda, ginger, cinnamon, allspice, cloves, salt, and black pepper. Set aside.

2. Using an electric mixer, beat ½ cup of the butter, ½ cup of the granulated sugar, and all of the brown sugar until light and fluffy, about 3 minutes, scraping down the sides of the bowl as necessary. Add the egg and beat for about 20 seconds, then scrape down the sides of the bowl. Add the molasses and beat until just combined, then scrape down the sides of the bowl again.

3. Add the dry ingredients, then mix on low speed until just incorporated. The dough will be very soft; refrigerate it for about 1 hour, or until firm enough to roll.

4. Preheat the oven to 350 degrees F and set a rack in the middle position. Line a baking sheet with parchment paper and set aside.

5. Place the remaining ½ cup of granulated sugar in a shallow bowl. Form the dough into 1-inch balls and roll in the sugar to coat. Place the balls on the prepared baking sheet about 2 inches apart.

6. Bake for 10 to 12 minutes, until set and golden on the outside and slightly soft on the inside. (As they bake, they will puff up and then flatten. Do not remove them from the oven until they are flat.) Let the cookies cool on the baking sheet for a few minutes, then transfer to a wire rack to cool completely. Refrigerate the dough between batches. The cookies will keep for several days in an airtight container. Freeze for longer storage.

INGREDIENTS

MAKES 36 COOKIES

2½ cups **all-purpose flour**, spooned into measuring cup and leveled off

2 teaspoons **baking soda**

2 teaspoons ground **ginger**

1 teaspoon ground **cinnamon**

½ teaspoon ground **allspice**

¼ teaspoon ground **cloves**

Scant ¼ teaspoon **salt**

Pinch freshly ground **black pepper**

2 sticks (1 cup) **unsalted butter**, softened but still cool

1 cup **granulated sugar**, divided

½ cup packed **light brown sugar**

1 large **egg**

⅓ cup **unsulphured molasses**

DECEMBER 27

ST. JOHN THE APOSTLE

— Israel —

Born: 2 or 6, Died: 100

St. John the Apostle, also known as John the Beloved and John the Evangelist, was one of Jesus' closest followers. A fisherman from Galilee and the brother of St. James the Greater, he was among the first disciples called by Christ, earning the title "son of thunder" (Mark 3:17). John witnessed many key moments in Jesus' ministry, including the Transfiguration and the agony in Gethsemane. At the Last Supper, he leaned on Jesus' chest, and at the Crucifixion, he alone remained with the women at the foot of the Cross, where Christ entrusted him with the care of His mother.

John is traditionally credited as the author of the Gospel of John, three epistles, and the book of Revelation. He survived persecution, including being thrown into boiling oil, and was exiled to the Isle of Patmos. He later returned to Ephesus, where he is believed to have died around A.D. 98. His feast on December 27 honors his steadfast faith and devotion. He is the patron of writers, scholars, and burn victims, among many others, and is venerated in dioceses and cities worldwide.

ST. JOHN'S WINE (MULLED WINE)

THIS MULLED WINE RECIPE IS A nod to the tradition of sharing blessed wine on the feast of St. John the Evangelist. It is said that St. John blessed a chalice of poisoned wine and drank it without being harmed. Because of this, the saint is often depicted in art holding a chalice with a snake emerging from it. There is even a prayer in the *Rituale Romanum* invoking the intercession of St. John for the blessing of wine.

Boil the spices in the wine in a large saucepan for about 5 minutes. Strain the wine. Serve hot.

INGREDIENTS

SERVES 6 TO 8

750-ml bottle medium- to full-bodied **red wine**

2 whole **cloves**

Two 2-inch **cinnamon sticks**

1 **cardamom pod**

½ teaspoon ground **nutmeg**

Cabernet Sauvignon, Zinfandel, Merlot, and Shiraz are all good options. Look for something with bold fruit flavors and a good balance of acidity and tannins.

Let Us Pray

Lord Jesus, help us ever to follow the example of Your holy family, that in the hour of our death Your glorious Virgin Mother together with St. Joseph may come to meet us, and we may be worthy to be received by You into the everlasting joys of Heaven. You live and reign forever. Amen.

SOLEMNITY OF THE HOLY FAMILY

FIRST SUNDAY AFTER CHRISTMAS

The Feast of the Holy Family celebrates Jesus, Mary, and Joseph as the perfect model of love, faith, and obedience. Though devotion to the Holy Family dates back centuries, the feast was first established in Canada in the early nineteenth century and later extended to the entire Church in 1920.

The Gospel of Matthew (2:13–15, 19–23) recounts the Holy Family's flight into Egypt, highlighting Joseph's unwavering trust in God's guidance. Warned in a dream, Joseph took Mary and Jesus to Egypt to escape Herod's wrath. After Herod's death, they returned to settle in Nazareth, fulfilling the prophecy that Jesus would be called a Nazorean.

This feast invites us to reflect on our own families, drawing inspiration from the Holy Family's virtues of love, faith, and trust in God's plan. It is a time to pray for our homes to be filled with the same light of mercy and salvation that shone from Nazareth.

SPINACH-LENTIL SOUP

THE MENTION OF LENTILS IN THE Old Testament suggests that these have been a favored ingredient in soups and stews, and it is likely that Mary prepared lentil-based dishes for the family. For generations since then, the four types of lentils—red, green, black, and brown—have been an esteemed source of fiber and protein. Today, numerous lentil-based recipes include salads, soups, and a traditional dish called mujadara, a combination of rice and lentils. It is unclear whether spinach was a staple vegetable in Jesus' time, but today spinach is popular in Israel.

1. In a large pot or Dutch oven, heat the oil over medium-high heat. Add the onion, carrots, celery, sweet potato cubes, and garlic. Sauté, stirring occasionally, until the vegetables are softened and golden, about 5 minutes.

2. Add the salt, red pepper flakes, cardamom, cumin, and cinnamon and sauté for another minute, stirring continuously to coat all vegetables with the spices.

3. Add the vegetable stock and lentils. Bring to a boil and reduce the heat to low. Cover and simmer until the lentils are tender, about 30 minutes, stirring occasionally. If the soup is too thick, add another ½ to 1 cup of stock.

4. Add the spinach and simmer for a few more minutes, or until the spinach wilts. Taste and season with black pepper. Ladle into soup bowls, and garnish with crumbled feta cheese and parsley.

INGREDIENTS

SERVES 6 TO 8

3–4 tablespoons **olive oil**

1 medium-sized **yellow onion**, peeled and diced

2 **carrots**, peeled and thinly sliced into rounds

2 **celery stalks**, cleaned and thinly sliced

1 large **sweet potato**, peeled and cut into cubes

4 cloves **garlic**, peeled and minced

1 teaspoon **salt**

¼ teaspoon crushed **red pepper flakes**

¼ teaspoon ground **cardamom**

¼ teaspoon ground **cumin**

¼ teaspoon ground **cinnamon**

2 quarts **low-sodium vegetable stock**

14-ounce or 16-ounce package **dried lentils** (about 2 ½ cups), rinsed

16 ounces fresh **baby spinach**, rinsed

Freshly ground **black pepper**, to taste

Feta cheese crumbles and fresh chopped **parsley**, for garnish

Let Us Pray

My soul proclaims the greatness of the Lord,
my spirit rejoices in God my Savior,
for he has looked with favor on his lowly servant.
From this day all generations will call me blessed:
the Almighty has done great things for me,
and holy is his Name.

SOLEMNITY OF MARY, MOTHER OF GOD

—Holy Day of Obligation —

JANUARY 1

January 1 is dedicated to Mary, honoring her as the Mother of God. This solemnity recognizes Mary as the Theotokos, a title affirmed at the Council of Ephesus in A.D. 431. Through her role in Christ's birth, Mary holds a central place in Christianity and is venerated under many names, including Blessed Virgin Mary, Queen of Heaven, and Our Lady.

Devotion to Mary has been a cornerstone of the Christian Faith for centuries. Countless prayers, feast days, and traditions celebrate her, and churches worldwide are dedicated in her honor. Pilgrims travel to Marian shrines, and many apparitions and miracles have been attributed to her.

Marian doctrines, such as her Immaculate Conception and bodily Assumption into Heaven, further emphasize her unique role in salvation history. Some traditions refer to Mary as the "New Eve," highlighting her participation in Christ's mission to redeem humanity.

One of the most profound prayers associated with Mary is the Magnificat (Luke 1:46–55), in which she proclaims, "My soul magnifies the Lord." This hymn of praise reflects Mary's deep faith and humility, making it a beautiful reflection for this feast day.

LADYFINGERS

THESE LIGHT, AIRY HOMEMADE LADYFINGERS FAR excel in delicacy and flavor the store-bought versions. Any leftovers after dessert should be well wrapped and can stay at room temperature for three days. Otherwise, wrap them tightly and freeze them for up to one month.

1. Preheat the oven to 325 degrees F. Line 2 baking sheets with parchment paper and set aside.

2. In a large mixing bowl or bowl of a stand mixer, combine the egg whites and cream of tartar and whisk the whites until soft peaks form. Slowly add ⅓ cup of sugar, continuing to whisk until the mixture is stiff and glossy. Set aside.

3. In another large bowl or bowl of a stand mixer, beat the egg yolks until well combined. Add the remaining sugar, vanilla, and salt and beat until the mixture becomes thick and pale yellow, about 4 to 5 minutes. When you stop beating, the mixture should fall from the beaters in ribbons as you lift them out of the bowl.

4. Sift the flour into the bowl, then fold gently until no flour remains. Fold the egg whites into the egg yolk mixture in 2 additions, mixing until just a few white streaks remain. Transfer the batter to a pastry bag fitted with a ⅜-inch to ½-inch plain round tip. Pipe the batter about 1 inch wide and 3 inches long onto the baking sheets. Space ladyfingers about 1 inch apart. You should be able to fit 2 dozen ladyfingers per baking sheet (piping 3 rows with 8 ladyfingers per row). Combine the confectioners' and granulated sugars and sift over the tops of the ladyfingers (it will be a generous dusting).

5. Bake the ladyfingers for 18 to 22 minutes, or until they are golden brown and spring back when gently touched. Allow the ladyfingers to cool for a few minutes on the sheets before carefully releasing them from the parchment with a flat spatula while they are still warm. After ladyfingers are released from the parchment, allow them to cool completely on the baking sheet.

INGREDIENTS

YIELDS ABOUT 4 DOZEN LADYFINGERS

6 large **eggs**, separated

½ teaspoon **cream of tartar**

⅔ cup **granulated sugar**, divided

2 teaspoons **pure vanilla extract**

½ teaspoon **table salt**

⅔ cup **all-purpose flour**

TOPPING:

¼ cup **confectioners' sugar**

2 tablespoons **granulated sugar**

Let Us Pray

Bless, O Lord God almighty, this home,
that in it there may be health, purity, the
strength of victory, humility, goodness
and mercy, the fulfillment of Thy law,
the thanksgiving to God the Father
and to the Son and to the Holy Spirit.
And may this blessing remain upon this
home and upon all who dwell herein.
Through Christ our Lord. Amen.

SOLEMNITY OF THE EPIPHANY

"THREE KINGS DAY"

JANUARY 6

*(In the USA, Catholics now celebrate Epiphany
on the first Sunday after January 1.)*

Epiphany, meaning "manifestation," is a major liturgical feast celebrating God's revelation to the world through the visit of the Magi. The Three Kings—Melchior, Caspar, and Balthazar—traveled to Bethlehem to honor the infant Jesus, recognizing Him as the Messiah for both Jews and Gentiles. Established around A.D. 361, Epiphany originally commemorated Christ's birth, His baptism, and the Adoration of the Magi.

Traditionally celebrated on January 6, twelve days after Christmas, Epiphany holds different traditions across Christian communities. In the Western Church, it marks Christ's manifestation to the Gentiles, while in the Eastern Church, it also commemorates His baptism by John the Baptist.

Spanish-speaking countries emphasize Jesus' kingship with regal imagery, and Orthodox Christians call the feast Theophany, focusing on His baptism.

Many cultures refer to this feast as Three Kings Day, celebrating the Magi's visit as a sign of salvation for all. Festivities include parades, church services, and family feasts, with some traditions extending the celebration for weeks.

A meaningful custom associated with Epiphany is the blessing of homes. In some places, a priest blesses households, but, when unavailable, the family's father may lead the blessing, invoking Christ's presence and protection for the coming year.

ROSCA DE REYES
THREE KINGS CAKE

ROSCA DE REYES IS A SWEET, ring-shaped bread enjoyed on Epiphany, flavored with hints of citrus zest and warm cinnamon. Often topped with candied fruits and a dusting of sugar, its rich, buttery dough pairs with the bright, jewel-like decorations to symbolize the gifts of the Magi.

1. To make the dough, heat the milk to a simmer in a small saucepan or at medium power in your microwave. Pour the hot milk over the butter, sugar, and salt, and stir occasionally until the butter melts. Cool the mixture to lukewarm.

2. In a mixing bowl, combine the milk mixture, eggs, and yeast. Measure the flour by gently spooning it into a cup, then leveling off any excess. Add the flour 1 cup at a time, mixing and kneading—by hand, bread machine, or stand mixer—until a soft, smooth dough forms.

3. Place the dough in a greased container, cover it, and let rise until doubled in size (about 1 to 1 ½ hours). Or let your bread machine complete the dough cycle.

4. After the first rise, deflate the dough, cover, and let it rest for 10 minutes. Turn the dough out onto a lightly floured surface; roll into a 20-inch x 12-inch rectangle.

5. To make the filling, brush the surface of the dough with the melted butter, leaving a ½-inch border bare along one of the long edges. Combine the sugar and cinnamon in a small bowl. Add the nuts, mixed fruits, and zest, and stir to coat. Sprinkle this mixture evenly over the buttered section of the dough.

INGREDIENTS

SERVES 16

DOUGH

⅔ cup **milk**

6 tablespoons **unsalted butter**, cold

⅓ cup **granulated sugar**

½ teaspoon **table salt**

2 large **eggs**, at room temperature

2 teaspoons **instant yeast**

3 ¼ cups **all-purpose flour**

FILLING

2 tablespoons **butter**, melted

2 tablespoons **granulated sugar**

½ teaspoon ground **cinnamon**

½ cup chopped **nuts**

¾ cup **dried mixed fruits**

1 tablespoon **lemon zest**, **orange zest**, or **lime zest**

GARNISH

Candied red cherries and/or candied orange peel

Almonds, pecans, cashews, or walnuts, toasted and sliced

6. To assemble, roll up the dough as you would a cinnamon roll, working toward the edge with no filling on it. Pinch the seam together to seal it firmly, then bring the ends together to form a ring. Grease the outside of a small bowl or ramekin and put it on a lightly greased or parchment-lined baking sheet. Place the ring, seam-side down, around the bowl. Pinch together the seam again where the two ends meet to ensure the ring is sealed.

7. Flatten the ring slightly, and using a pair of scissors, make cuts in the dough at 1 ½-inch intervals around the outside edge. If desired, hide a candy or almond (traditionally, figurines of the Christ Child were hidden) inside the dough — whoever finds it wins! Cover with greased plastic wrap and let rise until nearly doubled, about 30 to 40 minutes.

8. Once the dough is shaped and is rising for the second time, pre-heat the oven to 350 degrees F. When the dough is risen, remove the plastic wrap and brush the top with the egg wash. Place the candied cherries (cut in half) in the spaces between the slits in the dough and decorate with nuts as desired.

9. Bake the bread for 25 to 30 minutes, covering the loaf loosely with foil after the first 15 minutes, as it will brown quickly. Remove the bread from the oven when the inner parts of the slits look cooked and the interior measures 190 degrees F when measured with an instant-read thermometer. Cool the bread on a rack before slicing and serving.

Let Us Pray

"When Jesus was baptized, he went up immediately from the water, and behold, the heavens were opened and he saw the Spirit of God descending like a dove, and alighting on him; and lo, a voice from heaven, saying, 'This is my beloved Son, with whom I am well pleased.'" (Matt. 3:16–17)

THE BAPTISM
OF THE LORD

SUNDAY AFTER EPIPHANY

The Feast of the Baptism of the Lord, cele-brated after Epiphany, marks the moment when Jesus was baptized by John the Baptist in the Jordan River. This event, described in Matthew 3:13–17, reveals Christ's humility and divine mission.

Rather than proclaiming Himself as the Messiah, Jesus stood among sinners, awaiting baptism like everyone else. When John hesitated, saying, "I need to be baptized by you, and do you come to me?" Jesus responded, "Let it be so now; for thus it is fitting for us to fulfil all righteousness." As Jesus emerged from the water, the heavens opened, the Holy Spirit descended like a dove, and God's voice declared, "This is my beloved Son, with whom I am well pleased."

This feast highlights Christ's solidarity with humanity and the beginning of His public ministry. It also reminds us of the power of our own Baptism, calling us to live as beloved children of God, filled with His grace and mission.

SCALLOP SHELL SALAD WITH SARDINES

THE SCALLOP SHELL HAS BEEN A Christian symbol of Baptism for centuries, often depicted in sacred art as the vessel used to pour the water. In the early Church, clergy sometimes used actual scallop shells to anoint catechumens, reinforcing the connection between water, purification, and new life in Christ. As we celebrate the Baptism of the Lord—when Jesus sanctified the waters of the Jordan—this scallop shell pasta salad serves as a meaningful and refreshing dish, reminding us of our own baptismal call to follow Him.

1. Cook the pasta according to package instructions. Drain and rinse in cold water; cool and set aside. While the pasta is cooking, heat 1 ½ cups of water in a large saucepan, and add the kale. Simmer the kale for 8 to 10 minutes, drain, and set aside to cool. Once cool, dry off any remaining water.

2. Add the pasta to a large serving bowl, and add the sardines, chopped avocado, cherry tomatoes, mozzarella, corn kernels, and scallions. Stir well to combine, add the kale, and toss again.

3. Combine the olive oil, lime juice, mayonnaise, garlic powder, and salt, to taste, and stir together until well combined. Pour over the salad, toss, and serve.

INGREDIENTS

SERVES 6

1 pound **shell-shaped pasta**

12 ounces rinsed chopped **kale**

Two 3.5-ounce cans **sardines**, drained

1 ripe **avocado**, peeled, pit removed, and chopped

1 cup **cherry tomatoes**, rinsed and halved

½ pound **mozzarella**, cut into cubes

½ cup **corn kernels**

6 **scallions**, rinsed and chopped

4 tablespoons **olive oil**

4 tablespoons **lime juice**

2 tablespoons **mayonnaise**

1 teaspoon **garlic powder**

Salt, to taste

Ordinary Time
Between the Christmas Season and Lent

Let Us Pray

Our Father,
Who art in Heaven,
Hallowed be Thy name,
Thy Kingdom come, Thy will be done,
On earth as it is in Heaven.
Give us this day our daily bread,
And forgive us our trespasses
as we forgive those who trespass against us,
And lead us not into temptation,
But deliver us from evil. Amen.

ORDINARY TIME: BETWEEN THE CHRISTMAS SEASON AND LENT

Much of the liturgical calendar is made up of Ordinary Time. There are two periods of Ordinary Time during the year: between the end of the Christmas season and the beginning of Lent, and between the end of the Easter season and the beginning of Advent. In the rhythm of the Church's liturgical year, Ordinary Time may seem quiet, but it is anything but ordinary. This season invites us to grow in faith through the steady, day-to-day walk of discipleship. It is a time to reflect on Christ's teachings, deepen our relationship with Him, and sanctify the ordinary moments of life—including the meals we share around our tables.

In this cookbook, you'll find recipes that honor the spirit of Ordinary Time—wholesome, comforting, and deeply rooted in tradition. These meals celebrate the sacredness of everyday life, reminding us that even in the ordinary, God is present.

Ordinary Time is represented by the color green, which evokes life and hope. Dress your table in this fresh color. Add sprigs of leaves as centerpieces to your table.

Let Us Pray

Blessed are you, Lord God of
all creation. Through Your
goodness we have this candle to
light our way. As we celebrate
the Purification of Mary, help us
to purify our hearts, that we may
always walk in Your truth. Amen.

THE PRESENTATION
OF THE LORD

CANDLEMAS

FEBRUARY 2

Celebrated on February 2, Candlemas marks the Presentation of the Lord, also known as the Purification of the Blessed Virgin Mary or the Feast of the Holy Encounter. Traditionally, it concludes the Christmas and Epiphany seasons, symbolizing purification, renewal, and hope.

A key tradition of Candlemas is the blessing of candles, representing Christ as the Light of the World. Catholics, Eastern Orthodox, and some Protestant communities bring candles to church, where they are blessed in a solemn ceremony. The priest, clothed in purple, blesses and incenses the candles before distributing them to the faithful. Parishioners then process with their lit candles, symbolizing Christ's entry into the Temple of Jerusalem.

In keeping with tradition, the Canticle of Simeon (see Luke 2:29–32) is sung during the procession, reflecting Simeon's joyful recognition of Jesus as the promised Savior. In some churches, the celebration concludes with Marian hymns such as "Gaude Maria Virgo" or "Inviolata," honoring the Blessed Virgin.

This beautiful feast reminds the faithful that, just as Simeon and Anna recognized Jesus as the Messiah, we too are called to welcome Christ, the true Light, into our hearts and homes.

CANDLEMAS CRÊPES

In France, Candlemas (La Chandeleur) is traditionally celebrated with crêpes, their round, golden shape symbolizing both the returning light of Christ and the sun's renewal after winter. This custom dates back to at least the Middle Ages, when pilgrims visiting Rome for the Feast of the Presentation were given crêpes as a sign of blessing and prosperity. Enjoying these delicate pancakes on Candlemas connects us to this rich Christian tradition, reminding us of Christ, the Light of the World, and the warmth of His presence in our lives.

1. Sprinkle the thawed berries with 4 tablespoons of granulated sugar. Cover and refrigerate for several hours.

2. To make the crêpes, place the flour, milk, water, eggs, butter, granulated sugar, and the pinch of salt into a blender. Blend until well whipped. Pour the batter into a container with a pouring spout if your blender doesn't have one.

3. Heat a nonstick crêpe pan over medium-high heat. Spray the pan with nonstick cooking spray or melt a little bit of butter. When the pan is hot, pour 2 tablespoons of batter into the pan and rotate the pan until the bottom is coated with a thin—but not paper-thin—layer. Cook until the top is set and the bottom is lightly golden brown. Flip, using your finger or a spatula. Don't worry if this takes a few tries to get right.

4. After turning, cook until the other side is lightly browned. Remove from the pan and cool on parchment or wax paper. Place parchment or wax paper between each finished crêpe.

5. Whip the whipping cream with a mixer, adding confectioners' sugar and berry juice, until soft peaks form. To serve, place two crêpes on each plate. Place 2 to 3 tablespoons of whipped cream down the center of each. Roll each crêpe and place it seam-side down on the plate. Top with the berry-sugar mixture. Repeat with the remaining crêpes.

INGREDIENTS

SERVES 4 TO 6

1 bag frozen **mixed berries**, thawed

4 tablespoons **granulated sugar**

1 cup **all-purpose flour**

1 cup **whole milk**

½ cup **lukewarm water**

4 large **eggs**

4 tablespoons **butter**, melted

3 tablespoons **granulated sugar**

Pinch **salt**

1 ½ cups **whipping cream**

4 tablespoons **confectioners' sugar**

4 tablespoons **juice** from the sweetened berries to color the cream, or omit

If you don't have a crêpe pan, use a large nonstick skillet.

FEBRUARY 6

ST. PAUL MIKI

— Japan —

Born: circa 1562, Died: 1597

Born in 1562 near Osaka, Japan, St. Paul Miki converted to Christianity with his family and later joined the Jesuits. A gifted preacher, he was instrumental in converting many to the Faith. Just months before his ordination, he was arrested along with fellow Jesuits and Franciscans during a government crackdown on Christianity.

Condemned to crucifixion, the prisoners endured a brutal month-long march to Nagasaki, where they were mocked and tortured. Yet, Miki continued to preach, even as they approached their execution site. Upon seeing their crosses, they sang the Te Deum in thanksgiving. Tied to their crosses with iron bands, they were lifted up and pierced with lances. Paul Miki's final sermon, spoken from the cross, urged his listeners to embrace Christ.

Their martyrdom on February 6, 1597, sanctified Nagasaki's Nishizaka Hill. Today, St. Paul Miki is honored as the patron saint of Japan, a testament to unwavering faith in the face of persecution.

Being on February 6, this feast sometimes falls in the Lenten season.

EMBER DAY SHRIMP TEMPURA

1. To make the dipping sauce, whisk everything together in a saucepan over medium heat until sugar is dissolved. Set aside.

2. To prepare the shrimp, peel off all but the little fins, then devein and rinse them. Make small cuts about ¼ inch thick and ¼ inch apart across the inner curve of each shrimp. Stretch and squeeze with your fingers to flatten them out (you'll hear little popping sounds). Pat them dry, then use a sifter or mesh strainer to dust them lightly with flour on both sides.

3. To make the batter, measure 1 cup of the ice water (but no ice cubes) into a bowl. Use your chopsticks to beat the egg and combine it with the water. Add the flour and use chopsticks (not a whisk) to mix until the batter is combined but lumpy and the consistency of pancake batter.

4. Preheat the oil to 340 to 350 degrees F. Test the temperature with a thermometer or with chopsticks. When you see small bubbles form around a chopstick, it's ready for deep frying. Dip shrimp in the batter to coat. Lower each into the batter with chopsticks or tongs, moving it a bit at first to keep it from sticking to the bottom. Cook for 2 to 3 minutes, until crispy.

5. Cook two to four pieces at a time to keep from cooling the oil. Place on a paper towel on a baking tray to drain. Trays can be kept warm, on low, in the oven. Serve with rice and dipping sauce.

INGREDIENTS

SERVES 4

DIPPING SAUCE

¾ cup **dashi** or ¾ cup **water** plus 1 teaspoon **vegetable broth**

3 tablespoons **soy sauce**

2 tablespoons **mirin** or **dry white wine**

2 teaspoons **sugar**; double if using dry white wine

SHRIMP

1 pound **shrimp** or **prawns** (for best results, use 16–20 count per pound)

Flour, for dusting

Oil, for frying

TEMPURA BATTER

1 ½ cups **cold water with ice cubes**, divided

1 cold **egg**, beaten

1 cup **flour**, sifted

FEBRUARY 14

ST. VALENTINE

— Italy —

Born: Early third century,
Died: circa 270

The true identity of St. Valentine remains uncertain, as three different martyrs named Valentine were executed on February 14 in different years. The most well-known was a Roman priest and physician who comforted persecuted Christians under Emperor Claudius II. Arrested for his faith, he was beaten and beheaded in A.D. 270, buried along the Flaminian Way, and later honored with a basilica by Pope Julius.

Another Valentine was the bishop of Interamna (modern-day Terni), also martyred under Claudius II. A third Valentine died in Africa with his companions, though little is known about him. Despite their tragic fates, their legacy of faith and sacrifice endures.

Over time, St. Valentine became associated with love and devotion, possibly due to February's long-standing romantic traditions. Today, he is the patron saint of love, marriages, young people, travelers, and even beekeepers—an enduring symbol of steadfast faith and affection.

Being on February 14, this feast sometimes falls in the Lenten season.

VALENTINE'S DAY CAKE

THIS DECADENT VALENTINE'S DAY CAKE IS a perfect way to share joy with family
and friends, reminding us of the sacrificial love at the heart of this saint's legacy.
Bake with love, serve with gratitude, and enjoy a dessert fit for a feast day!

1. Preheat the oven to 350 degrees F. Butter a round cake pan and line it with parchment paper. Butter and flour the parchment paper and set the pan aside.

2. In a medium bowl, sift together the all-purpose flour and baking powder. In another bowl, cream the butter and sugar. Add the beaten eggs, alternating with the sifted flour and baking powder.

3. Pour the batter into the prepared cake pan, and bake until the cake is springy to the touch and golden brown, about 40 minutes. Transfer to a wire rack to cool.

4. While the cake is cooling, make the raspberry syrup. In a small saucepan, combine the sugar and ½ cup water; bring to a boil over medium-high heat. Cook, stirring occasionally, until the sugar has completely dissolved. Stir in the framboise and set the pot over a basin of ice. Stir occasionally until completely chilled.

5. To make the whipped cream, combine the cream, sugar, and vanilla in a medium bowl. Beat at high speed until soft peaks form, about 5 minutes.

6. Once the cake is cool, turn the cake out onto a cutting board, and carefully peel the bottom layer of parchment paper off the bottom. Using a serrated knife, cut the cake in half horizontally. Brush the cut sides of the cake liberally with the raspberry syrup. Spread half of the whipped cream onto the bottom layer. Cover the cream with an even layer of raspberries. Spread the remaining whipped cream over the berries. Place the top of the cake cut side down over the cream. Dust the top with confectioners' sugar.

INGREDIENTS
SERVES 8 TO 10

1 ¾ cups (3 ½ sticks) **unsalted butter**, melted

1 cup **superfine sugar**

6 **eggs**

2 cups **all-purpose flour**, sifted

2 level teaspoons **baking powder**

1 teaspoon **vanilla extract**

Raspberry syrup (see below)

Whipped cream (see below)

2 pints fresh **raspberries**

Confectioners' sugar, for dusting

RASPBERRY SYRUP

½ cup **granulated sugar**

2 teaspoons **framboise** (see note)

WHIPPED CREAM

2 cups **heavy cream**

2 tablespoons **confectioners' sugar**

1 teaspoon **vanilla extract**

Framboise is a raspberry-flavored liqueur, but as an alternative, you can heat a spoonful of raspberry jam until it becomes watery.

SHROVE TUESDAY, TUESDAY BEFORE ASH WEDNESDAY

While not part of Lent, Shrove Tuesday is deeply connected to the Lenten season and has a long culinary tradition in the Church. As the final day before the Lenten fast, Shrove Tuesday has become a day of feasting and even a time for parades and festivals, such as Mardi Gras in New Orleans. In many European countries, it is also known as "Pancake Day," and pancakes have become a traditional food on this day before Lent.

Not only a day for feasting and culinary delights — it is known as "Fat Tuesday," after all — Shrove Tuesday has also historically been tied to the Lenten season through the observance of the sacrament of Reconciliation. Derived from the Old English word *scrīfan*, "shrove" means to hear confession and give the sacrament of Penance, in this case in preparation for the upcoming forty days of Lent.

BUTTERMILK PANCAKES

Shrove Tuesday has long been associated with pancakes, a tradition that dates back to medieval Europe when Christians used up rich ingredients like eggs, milk, and butter before the Lenten fast.

1. In a large bowl, combine the flour, sugar, baking powder, baking soda, and salt. In a separate bowl, beat together the buttermilk, milk, eggs, and melted butter. Keep the two mixtures separate until you are ready to cook.

2. Heat a lightly oiled griddle or frying pan over medium-high heat. To check if the pan is hot enough, flick some water onto the surface—it should bead up and sizzle.

3. Pour the wet mixture into the dry mixture and mix until just combined; do not overmix. Pour or scoop the batter onto the griddle, using approximately ½ cup for each pancake. Brown on both sides. Serve hot with butter and maple syrup!

INGREDIENTS

SERVES 4 TO 6

3 cups **all-purpose flour**

3 tablespoons **granulated sugar**

3 teaspoons **baking powder**

1 ½ teaspoons **baking soda**

¾ teaspoon **salt**

3 cups **buttermilk**

½ cup **milk**

3 **eggs**

1/3 cup **butter**, melted

Melted butter, for serving

Maple syrup, for serving

FEASTS AND SOLEMNITIES

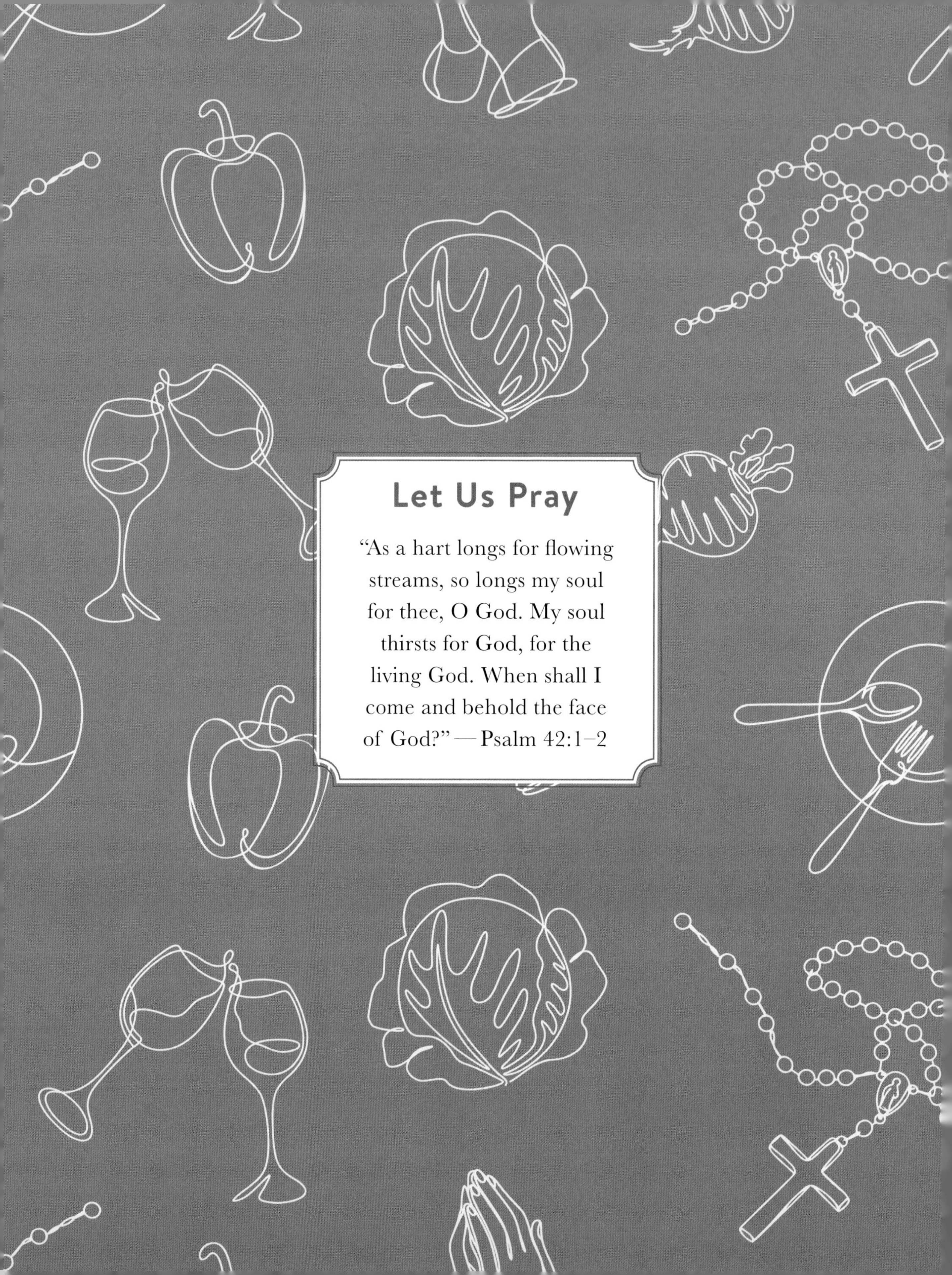

Let Us Pray

"As a hart longs for flowing streams, so longs my soul for thee, O God. My soul thirsts for God, for the living God. When shall I come and behold the face of God?" — Psalm 42:1–2

LENT

Lent, the season leading up to Easter, is marked by fasting, prayer, and penance, reflecting its roots as one of the most ancient and culturally significant observances in Christian tradition. This period of forty days, established by the Council of Nicaea in 325, serves multiple spiritual purposes: preparation for Easter, preparation for Baptism, and commemoration of Jesus Christ's desert fast. Historically, Lent was a time when the faithful engaged in strict fasting regimes, such as the Black Fast in the West and *xerophagy* in the East, which included abstaining from meat, fish, eggs, dairy, oil, and wine.

The essence of Lent is not merely about physical deprivation but involves a deeper, spiritual journey aimed at renewing focus on Christ, particularly the suffering Christ. This duality embodies Lent's paradox — the mourning of Christ's suffering juxtaposed with the joy derived from the foreknowledge of His Resurrection. Fasting during Lent is thus seen not only as a form of physical discipline but as a means to spiritual enlightenment, reminding believers of the transient nature of earthly life and the promise of eternal life with God.

Lent also emphasizes communal and personal practices, where traditional fasts are complemented by acts of charity and intensified prayer. Modern observances may be less austere, but they maintain the core principle: a voluntary surrender to a period of scarcity, intended to foster spiritual growth and a closer relationship with God. This adaptive practice continues to evolve, offering an opportunity for believers to reengage with its spiritual intents and reimagine its application in contemporary life.

As in Advent, the liturgical color for Lent is violet or purple. These two seasons of preparation for important events in our Christian Faith share the same color and even some of the same habits of penance and reflection.

THE BLACK FAST

Hitherto we have fasted only until none [3 p.m.], whereas, now [during Lent]
kings and princes, clergy and laity, rich and poor will fast until evening.

—St. Bernard

The Black Fast is the most rigorous form of fasting in the history of the Church. Not only does the Black Fast limit the content and quantity of food eaten, but also the time during which the penitent can eat. Here are the basic rules for the Black Fast:

✠ The penitent can eat only one meal per day.

✠ The penitent cannot eat flesh meat, eggs, butter, cheese, or milk nor drink wine.

✠ During Holy Week, the penitent can only eat bread, salt, and herbs and drink water.

✠ The penitent can eat their one meal only after sunset.

Fasting practices have evolved during the history of the Church, but those Catholics who wish to engage in the same timeless traditions of the Church as the early Christians might wish to practice the Black Fast. This fast is not encouraged for young children, the elderly, or anyone suffering from poor health.

INFORMATION ON THE BLACK FAST WAS adapted from The Catholic Encyclopedia (O'Neill, James David, "The Black Fast." The Catholic Encyclopedia, Vol. 2. [New York: Robert Appleton Company, 1907], www.newadvent.org/cathen/02590c.htm.)

TRADITIONAL FASTING SUBSTITUTION LIST

BUTTER/GHEE

✚ Oil, such as sunflower, canola, sesame, coconut, olive, etc. (1:1).

✚ For baking: 1 cup of pureed avocado replaces 1 cup of butter.

BUTTERMILK

✚ Add 1 tablespoon of vinegar to any of the milk substitutes (1:1).

CREAM

✚ Coconut cream (1:1).

✚ Silken tofu and soy milk; blend equal parts together (1:1).

EGGS

✚ Hydrated flax meal or chia seeds (1:1); replace 1 egg by mixing 1 tablespoon of ground flax meal or chia seeds with 3 tablespoons of water and let sit for 15 minutes until it forms a gel-like substance.

✚ Aquafaba, a brine strained from beans, most commonly chickpeas (3:1, 2:1 for egg white); use 3 tablespoons of aquafaba per egg or 2 tablespoons per egg white. This can even be whipped to make meringue.

✚ Applesauce ¼ cup (1:1).

✚ Banana ½ ripe, mashed (1:1).

✚ Silken tofu ¼ cup, pureed (1:1).

MILK

✚ Plain, unsweetened plant or nut milk, such as soy, almond, rice, or oat (1:1).

PARMESAN

✚ Nutritional yeast (1:1).

WHIPPED CREAM

✚ Both of the substitutions for cream can also be whipped for whipped cream (1:1).

YOGURT

✚ Non-dairy yogurt, such as soy, almond, cashew, or coconut (1:1). If the recipe calls for Greek yogurt, simply choose a Greek-style non-dairy yogurt.

ASH WEDNESDAY

Ash Wednesday marks the beginning of the Lenten Season. At each Ash Wednesday Mass, the priest uses the ashes from burnt palms from the last year's Easter Vigil and rubs an ashen cross on the forehead of each parishioner. His words are, "Remember that you are dust, and to dust you shall return." The cross is a symbol that acknowledges sin and reminds people to do penance for past sins.

For Catholics, Ash Wednesday is also a day of fasting and abstinence. According to the USCCB, Catholics from age eighteen to fifty-nine are "permitted to eat one full meal, as well as two smaller meals that together are not equal to a full meal." The law concerning abstinence is binding for all Catholics from age fourteen onward.

GEORGANN'S SPINACH QUICHE

THIS SIMPLE QUICHE IS A DELICIOUS substitute for a meat-based meal on Ash Wednesday and may become so popular that it will be a standard dinner meal throughout the year.

1. Preheat the oven to 425 degrees F.

2. Heat the butter in a skillet over medium heat. Sauté the onions and the garlic for 3 to 5 minutes. Combine the eggs, cream, salt, nutmeg, and cayenne pepper in a bowl, and beat to mix thoroughly. Spread the onion and garlic mixture across the bottom of the pie shell. Then spread the spinach over the onion-garlic mixture—it will float to the top while baking. Spread the grated cheese over the spinach. Pour the egg mixture over the top.

3. Bake for 15 minutes and then reduce the heat to 350 degrees F and bake for 30 minutes longer, or until golden brown. Remove from the oven and serve hot.

INGREDIENTS

SERVES 3 TO 4

2 tablespoons **butter**

2 tablespoons peeled and minced **onion**

2 large cloves **garlic**, peeled and minced

4 large **eggs**

1 cup **light cream**

½ teaspoon **salt**

½ teaspoon ground **nutmeg**

½ teaspoon ground **cayenne pepper**

1 cup chopped **spinach**, blanched and well drained

½ cup grated **Swiss cheese**

1 (9-inch) ready-made deep-dish **pie shell**

MARCH 17

ST. PATRICK

— Ireland —

Born: circa 385, Died: circa 461

St. Patrick, the patron saint of Ireland, is celebrated on March 17, the presumed date of his death. Though now synonymous with the Emerald Isle, he was actually born in Roman Britain in the late third century, with the birth name Maewyn Succat. At age sixteen, he was kidnapped by Irish pirates and enslaved as a shepherd. In captivity, he turned to God, and after six years, he escaped back to Britain following a divine vision.

Years later, Patrick had another revelation calling him to return to Ireland as a missionary. After years of religious training, he was ordained a priest and sent to convert the Irish. He skillfully merged Christian teachings with local traditions, famously using the three-leafed shamrock to explain the Holy Trinity.

Though never formally canonized, Patrick is revered for spreading Christianity across Ireland. Today, he is honored not only in Ireland but worldwide, celebrated with parades, festivals, and the wearing of green.

BEEF AND GUINNESS PIE

I N HONOR OF S T. P ATRICK'S FEAST day, this hearty Beef and Guinness Pie celebrates the robust flavors of Ireland's iconic stout and comforting pub fare. It's a fitting tribute to the great saint and a delicious way to gather around the table for a festive Irish meal.

1. To make the pastry, in a large bowl, add the flour, salt, and butter. With your fingers or a pastry blender, work the butter into the flour until it is the texture of fine breadcrumbs. Work as quickly as possible to avoid warming the dough.

2. Add 2 tablespoons of very cold water, stirring it into the dough using a cold knife until it binds together and can be formed into a ball. If it becomes too dry, add more water, 1 teaspoon at a time. Wrap the ball of dough in plastic wrap. Chill in the refrigerator for at least 15 minutes or up to 30 minutes.

3. To make the filling, in a large bowl, add the flour and season it with salt and ground black pepper. Add the cubes of meat and toss well in the flour until evenly coated.

4. In a large skillet or Dutch oven, heat the butter and oil over medium-high heat until the butter has melted. Add the meat to the fat in small batches and brown quickly all over for just a minute, then remove with a slotted spoon and set aside. Add the onions and carrots to the pan and fry gently for about 2 minutes. Return the meat to the pan, and add the Guinness, hot beef stock, Worcestershire sauce, tomato purée, and sugar. Season with salt and freshly ground black pepper, stir well, and bring to a boil.

INGREDIENTS

SERVES 4 TO 6

PASTRY

½ cup **all-purpose flour**

1 pinch **salt**

½ cup **unsalted butter**, cubed, or an equal mix of butter and lard

3 tablespoons **cold water**

FILLING

¼ cup **all-purpose flour**

Kosher salt, to taste

Freshly ground **black pepper**, to taste

2 pounds **chuck steak**, cut into 1-inch cubes

About ¼ cup **unsalted butter**

1 tablespoon **vegetable oil**

2 large **onions**, peeled and thinly sliced

2 large **carrots**, cut into 1-inch cubes

1 pint (2 cups) **Guinness**, or other **stout beer**

5. Cover, reduce to a gentle simmer, and cook slowly for about 2 hours, or until the meat is tender and the sauce has thickened and is glossy. Remove from the heat, place into a 9-inch pie dish, and leave to cool completely.

6. Preheat the oven to 400 degrees F. Roll out the pastry to ⅛-inch thick. Cut a ¾-inch strip from the rolled-out pastry. Brush the rim of the pie dish with water and place the pastry strip around the rim, pressing it down.

7. Cut out the remaining pastry about 1-inch larger than the pie dish. If you have one, place a pie funnel (also called a pie bird) in the center of the filling to support the pastry and prevent it from becoming soggy. Place the pastry lid over the top and press down to the edge and seal. Trim off any excess pastry and crimp the edges with a fork or between your thumb and forefinger. If you are not using a pie funnel, cut three small vents into the pastry lid. Brush the top with the beaten egg and make a hole in the center to reveal the pie funnel. You can also decorate the top of the pie with pastry trimmings as you like.

8. Bake for 30 to 35 minutes until the pastry is crisp and golden. Remove from the oven and serve hot.

1 ¼ cups hot **beef stock**

2 teaspoons **Worcestershire sauce**

2 teaspoons **tomato purée**

2 teaspoons **granulated sugar**

2 tablespoons **water**

1 large **egg**, beaten

Let Us Pray

Remember, O most chaste spouse of the Virgin Mary, that never was it known that anyone who implored your help and sought your intercession were left unassisted. Full of confidence in your power I fly unto you and beg your protection. Despise not O Guardian of the Redeemer my humble supplication, but in your bounty, hear and answer me. Amen.

SOLEMNITY OF ST. JOSEPH

MARCH 19

The Feast of St. Joseph, celebrated on March 19, is a beloved solemnity in the Catholic Church, honoring St. Joseph, the foster father of Jesus and patron of the universal Church. As the model of humility, obedience, and unwavering trust in God, St. Joseph has long been venerated by the faithful. His feast day is especially dear to Italians, Sicilians, and various Catholic communities worldwide, marked by rich traditions of prayer, charity, and, of course, food.

The origins of St. Joseph's feast date back to the Middle Ages, when, according to tradition, the people of Sicily prayed for his intercession during a severe famine. When the rains finally came, they celebrated in gratitude with a grand feast. This tradition gave rise to the St. Joseph's Table (*La Tavola di San Giuseppe*)—a communal offering of meatless dishes, symbolizing both abundance and humility.

In keeping with the Lenten season, St. Joseph's feast features vegetarian fare, with classic dishes like *pasta con le sarde* (pasta with sardines), fava beans, minestrone, and rich breads shaped like crosses and lilies. Desserts also hold a special place, particularly *zeppole*, pastries filled with custard or ricotta. The fava bean, once a famine staple, remains a symbol of St. Joseph's intercession.

For Catholics, this feast is more than just a meal—it is a spiritual gathering of gratitude, recalling St. Joseph's quiet strength and faithfulness. Whether through traditional dishes or prayers for his intercession, celebrating St. Joseph's feast invites us to reflect on his example as protector, provider, and saintly father.

ZEPPOLE DI SAN GIUSEPPE

ZEPPOLE IS A TRADITIONAL ITALIAN DESSERT popular in pastry shops all across Italy. With slight differences depending on the type of cream used, it is not only popular for celebrating St. Joseph's Day (which in Italy is also Father's Day) but also is used for carnival celebrations and for home desserts.

1. Preheat the oven to 400 degrees F. Line a baking sheet with parchment paper and set it aside.

2. To make the pastry, add the water, butter, and sugar in a medium-sized saucepan and place it over medium heat. Cook until it comes to a boil. Add the flour all at once and stir vigorously with a whisk for about 1 minute, or until the mixture forms a ball.

3. Remove from the heat and keep stirring to cool the dough. When cooled slightly, add an egg and beat well until well incorporated. Add the next and repeat with the remaining eggs until the batter is smooth and glossy.

4. Spoon small puffs about 3 inches round onto the baking sheet. Poke a small hole in the center of the upper part of each of the pastry puffs.

5. Bake for about 30 minutes. Turn off the oven and leave for 10 minutes. Remove from the oven and place on a cooling rack.

6. While the cream puffs are baking, make the pastry cream. Place the egg yolks into a medium-sized saucepan. Add the sugar and cornstarch and whisk together until uniform. When the mixture is smooth, place the saucepan on the stove over low heat. Begin pouring in the warm milk, whisking constantly. Turn the heat up to medium. Continue whisking and gradually increase the heat. The pastry cream will thicken as the heat rises.

7. When the mixture comes to a boil, let it cook for about 3 minutes, then remove from the heat. Add the vanilla and keep stirring as it cools so that it doesn't form a skin. Move into a large bowl and set the bowl into a larger bowl with ice water. Cover and refrigerate the filling until completely chilled.

8. To finish, using a piping bag, poke a hole into the side of each zeppole and fill with pastry cream. Pipe some pastry cream on top of each and dust with confectioners' sugar.

INGREDIENTS

SERVES 16

PASTRY

1 cup **water**

½ cup **butter**, at room temperature

1 teaspoon **granulated sugar**

1 cup **all-purpose flour**

4 **eggs**, at room temperature

Confectioners' sugar for decoration

PASTRY CREAM

4 **egg yolks**

⅓ cup **granulated sugar**

3 tablespoons plus 1 teaspoon **cornstarch**

Pinch **salt**

1 ¾ cups **whole milk**, warmed

1 teaspoon **vanilla extract**

Let Us Pray

Pour forth, we beseech Thee, O Lord, Thy grace into our hearts; that we, to whom the incarnation of Christ, Thy Son, was made known by the message of an angel, may by His Passion and Cross be brought to the glory of His Resurrection, through the same Christ Our Lord. Amen.

SOLEMNITY OF THE ANNUNCIATION

MARCH 25

The Feast of the Annunciation, celebrated on March 25, marks the moment when the Angel Gabriel appeared to Mary, announcing that she would conceive and bear the Son of God (see Luke 1:26–38). Mary's humble and faithful response, "Behold, I am the handmaid of the Lord; let it be to me according to your word," demonstrated her acceptance of God's will. This event is central to Christian belief, as it marks the Incarnation—when the Word became flesh in Mary's womb.

The Annunciation has long been revered, inspiring centuries of devotion, art, and liturgical traditions. The Magnificat (see Luke 1:46–55), Mary's song of praise, has been recited in evening prayers (Vespers) by clergy and religious communities for generations.

Known in many countries as "Lady Day" or "Our Lady's Day," this solemn feast has been celebrated with great reverence. In medieval Rome, vibrant processions honored Mary, culminating in a papal Mass where gold was gifted to impoverished brides. In Russia, tradition held that even birds would not mate on this holy day. From Renaissance paintings to iconography, the Annunciation continues to inspire faith and devotion worldwide.

It would be nice to pray the Angelus this day. The prayer is traditionally said at 6 a.m., noon, and 6 p.m. It would be fitting to pray it before dinner as a family.

FEAST OF THE ANNUNCIATION SWEDISH WAFFLES

THE SWEDISH HAVE ESTABLISHED A TRADITION for the Feast of the Annunciation that they have called "Waffle Day." It turns out that what was once called "Our Lady's Day" sounds like the Swedish word, *Våffeldagen*. That translates as "waffle day," and today, the once square-shaped waffles are now heart shaped and served with jams or fruits such as lingonberries, plus whipped cream or ice cream. These thin waffles have a pancake-like texture. A standard waffle iron is fine to use.

1. Sift the flour and salt into a large bowl. Fold in the sour cream and the water together.

2. Keep this batter in the refrigerator for 1 to 2 hours. Add the melted butter to the batter. Heat the waffle iron and cook according to the manufacturer's instructions. Serve with lemon juice, sugar, and cinnamon, or stewed lingonberries.

INGREDIENTS

SERVES 4 TO 6

1 ⅓ cups **all-purpose flour**

½ teaspoon **salt**

1 ½ teaspoons **sugar**

½ cup **sour cream**

½ cup **ice water**

½ cup **butter**, melted

Toppings: **lemon juice, sugar, cinnamon, or stewed lingonberries**

Holy Week

Scripture Reading

[Jesus said] "I give you a new commandment, that you love one another. Just as I have loved you, you also should love one another. By this everyone will know that you are my disciples, if you have love for one another." — John 13:34-35

HOLY WEEK

oly Week marks the pinnacle of the Catholic liturgical year, commemorating the Passion, Death, and Resurrection of Christ. It begins with Christ's triumphal entry into Jerusalem on Palm Sunday, followed by the solemnity of Holy Thursday night, the sorrow of Good Friday, the stillness of Holy Saturday, and, finally, the joy of Easter Sunday. The entire week is an invitation to enter deeply into the most profound and saving mysteries of the Faith.

There are many devotions that the faithful are invited to participate in during this solemn week. Most parishes offer an evening Mass on Holy Thursday, celebrating the institution of the Eucharist. Good Friday, that most somber day, is normally observed—together with the requisite fasting and abstinence—by participating in the Stations of the Cross or by attending the Good Friday service at the local parish. The faithful are encouraged to attend the Easter Vigil Mass on Holy Saturday evening, the most sacred and solemn Mass of the liturgical year. Fair warning, it's regularly more than three hours long!

Holy Week not only anchors our faith; it also invites us into a deeper understanding of Christ's ultimate act of love and obedience to God's will. His sacrifice established the New Covenant, foretold in the Old Testament, marking a renewal for all humanity. As we partake in these sacred days, let us open our hearts to the transformative power of Christ's Passion, Death, and Resurrection.

Scripture Reading

" 'Hosanna! Blessed is he who comes in the
name of the Lord! Blessed is the kingdom
of our father David that is coming!
Hosanna in the highest!' " —Mark 11:9–10

PASSION (PALM) SUNDAY

Palm Sunday marks Christ's triumphant entry into Jerusalem, the beginning of Holy Week. As He rode a humble donkey, crowds gathered, laying cloaks and palm branches before Him, joyfully shouting, "Hosanna to the Son of David! Blessed is he who comes in the name of the Lord!" (Matt. 21:9).

This moment fulfilled Old Testament prophecies, signifying Jesus as the true King—not one of earthly power, but of divine salvation. He entered the city not to claim a throne but to embrace the Cross, beginning His journey toward the ultimate sacrifice for humanity.

Many churches commemorate it with processions and the blessing of palm branches, continuing a tradition that echoes the voices of Jerusalem welcoming the Savior.

FIG-ARUGULA SALAD WITH GOAT CHEESE

On Palm Sunday, we recall Christ's entry into Jerusalem, greeted with palms and anticipation. The pairing of sweet figs and bitter arugula reflects the complex emotions of this day — celebration tinged with the foreknowledge of Christ's impending sacrifice.

1. Put the arugula into a salad bowl. Add the remaining ingredients, tossing lightly to combine.

2. In a small bowl, whisk together the apple cider vinegar, lime juice, garlic, Dijon mustard, sugar, and salt and pepper, to taste. Slowly drizzle in the olive oil while whisking continuously until fully incorporated and emulsified.

3. Drizzle the dressing over the salad and toss to combine.

INGREDIENTS

SERVES 4

SALAD

2 cups **baby arugula**, rinsed

5 **dried figs**, stemmed, peeled, and quartered.

4 ounces **goat cheese**, diced

1 **avocado**, diced

½ cup diced **red onion**

½ cup shelled **pistachios**

DRESSING

¼ cup **olive oil**, preferably extra virgin

1 teaspoon **apple cider vinegar**

1 teaspoon **lime juice**

1 teaspoon minced **garlic**

1 teaspoon **Dijon mustard**

1 teaspoon **granulated sugar**

Salt and freshly ground **black pepper**, to taste

Scripture Reading

"And he took bread, and when he had given thanks he broke it and gave it to them, saying, 'This is my body which is given for you. Do this in remembrance of me.' And likewise the cup after supper, saying, 'This cup which is poured out for you is the new covenant in my blood.'" —Luke 22:19–20

HOLY (MAUNDY) THURSDAY

Maundy Thursday is a sacred day that draws us into the heart of Holy Week, commemorating the Last Supper — the institution of the Eucharist. On this night, Jesus gathered with His disciples, broke bread, and shared the cup, declaring, "This is my body … this is my blood" (Mark 14.22, 24). With these words, He gave us the greatest gift — the Holy Eucharist, the source and summit of our Faith.

As we prepare to enter the Triduum, Maundy Thursday invites us to reflect on the deep mystery of the Eucharist and the sacrifice of Christ on the Cross. Many Catholics observe this day by attending Mass, adoring the Blessed Sacrament, and sharing a simple yet meaningful meal in remembrance of that sacred supper nearly two thousand years ago.

According to historians, a traditional seder meal would include the stew dish cholent, roasted lamb, olives with hyssop, bitter herbs (such as watercress and parsley), fruit-and-nut paste, likely with dried figs or dates, and matzo bread. What Christ ate at the Last Supper has not been confirmed, but it was likely a traditional Passover meal. And the bread used at the institution of the Eucharist was matzo, or unleavened bread.

UNLEAVENED BREAD OR MATZO

MODERN VERSIONS OF THE MATZO THAT Christ ate at the Last Supper are eaten at Passover seders to remember the Jewish flight from Egypt. As the recipe donor noted, you can spice up your matzo by adding chopped onion, minced garlic, or fresh herbs to your dough prior to baking.

1. Preheat the oven to 450 degrees F. Grease a sheet pan and set it aside.

2. Combine all ingredients with the water to form a dough and knead for about 3 minutes. Divide into 8 balls. Flatten each into a thin round and dock with a fork.

3. Bake for 10 minutes, cool, and serve.

INGREDIENTS

SERVES 8

2 cups **whole wheat flour, hard white wheat** or **spelt**

½ cup **cold water**

¼ cup **olive oil**

1 teaspoon **salt**

Scripture Reading

"He said, 'It is finished'; and he bowed his head and gave up his spirit." —John 19:30

GOOD FRIDAY

Good Friday is the most solemn day of the liturgical year, marking the Crucifixion and death of Jesus Christ. It is a day of deep reflection, fasting, and prayer, calling us to remember Christ's ultimate sacrifice for our salvation. As Catholics, we approach Good Friday with reverence, participating in the Stations of the Cross, venerating the Cross, and embracing acts of penance.

In stark contrast to the celebratory nature of most feast days, Good Friday is a day of abstinence and fasting. The Church calls upon the faithful to reflect on the gravity of sin and the immensity of Jesus' atonement.

In this observance, we turn to foods that embody simplicity and humility, avoiding the opulence that characterizes other celebrations. Traditional meals are typically sparse, with many choosing to partake in simple bread and water as a form of spiritual communion with the suffering of Christ.

This day invites us to quiet our hearts, to enter into the mystery of Christ's Passion, and to prepare for the joy of His Resurrection. As we gather around the table for a modest meal, we remember that even in suffering, God's love nourishes us, sustaining both body and soul.

The liturgical color for Good Friday is red, to mark Christ's Passion and death. Dress the table with red linens or dinnerware if you have them.

CREAMY CORN CHOWDER WITH SHRIMP

HUMBLE AND NUTRITIOUS, THIS CORN CHOWDER is the perfect meal to share with your family on this solemn day. The addition of seafood makes for a unique take on an American classic. Corn chowder is actually a historic American recipe first published back in the last 1800s in the *Boston Cook Book* by Mary Lincoln.

1. Heat the butter in a large stockpot over medium heat. When the butter is melted, stir in the onion, yellow bell pepper, and garlic and sweat for 5 to 10 minutes, until the vegetables are tender. Sprinkle the flour over the vegetables and stir well.

2. Stir in the heavy cream, and when smooth, add the corn and continue to cook over medium-low heat for 1 to 2 minutes.

3. Add the shrimp and stir, cooking until the shrimp turn pink, about 5 to 7 minutes. Season with salt and pepper, to taste.

4. Serve while hot and garnish with the chopped scallions, chopped parsley, and parmesan cheese.

INGREDIENTS

SERVES 4 TO 6

2 tablespoons **butter**

1 medium **onion**, peeled and diced

1 **yellow bell pepper**, seeded and diced

2 cloves **garlic**, peeled and diced

2 tablespoons **flour**

2 ½ cups **heavy cream**

15-ounce can **creamed corn**

1 pound peeled and deveined **shrimp**, raw

Salt and freshly ground **black pepper,** to taste

3 whole **scallions**, thinly chopped, for garnish

1 cup chopped **parsley**, for garnish

1 cup shredded **parmesan cheese**, for garnish

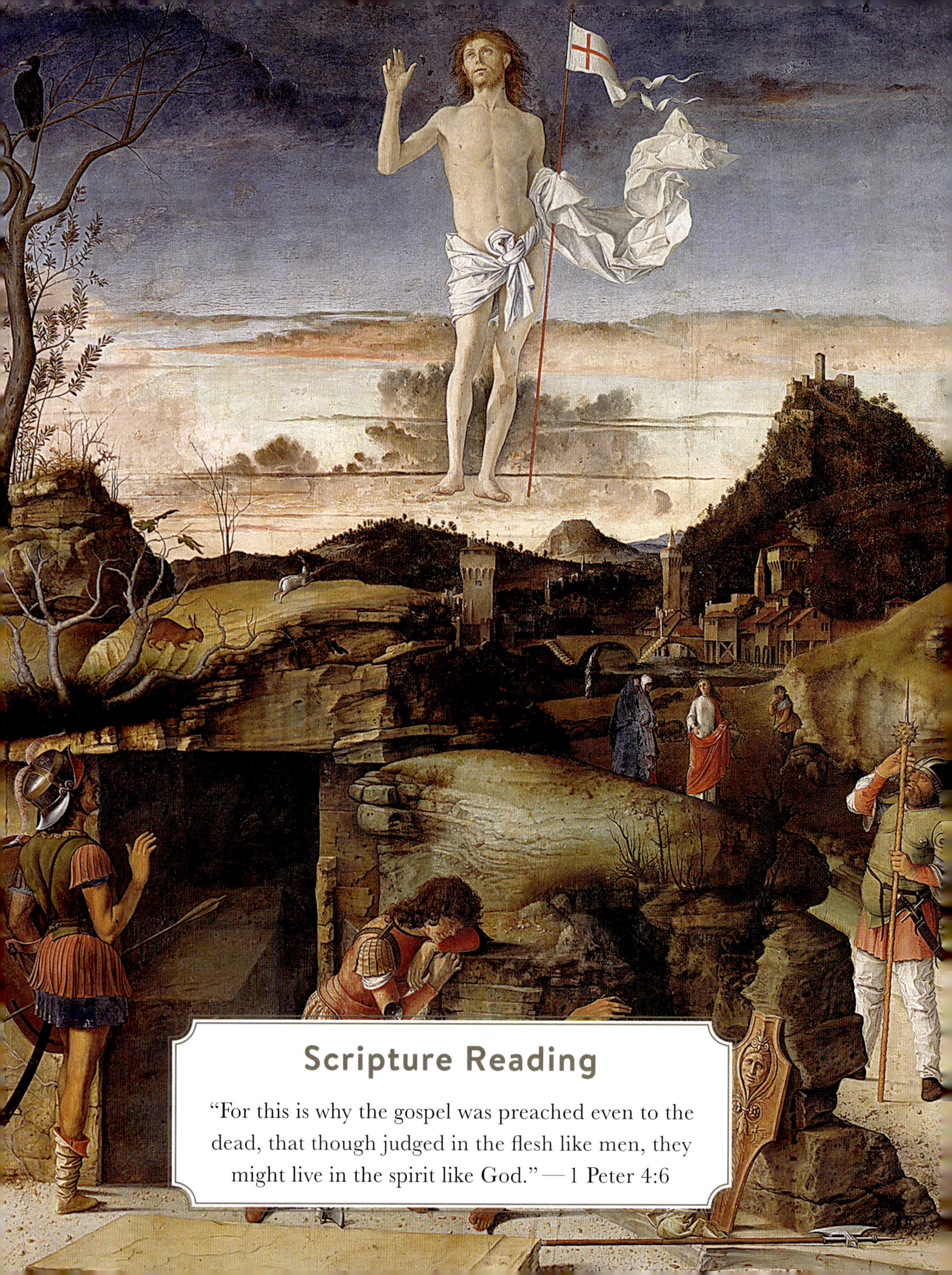
Scripture Reading

"For this is why the gospel was preached even to the dead, that though judged in the flesh like men, they might live in the spirit like God." — 1 Peter 4:6

HOLY SATURDAY

Holy Saturday is a day of silence, waiting, and deep anticipation. The sorrow of Good Friday lingers, yet the hope of Easter is near. It is the day Christ lay in the tomb, and the world held its breath, longing for the promise of the Resurrection to be fulfilled. For Catholics, this is a day of quiet reflection, a time to prepare our hearts for the joy that is to come.

Traditionally, Holy Saturday is a day of fasting and prayer, much like Good Friday. The Church, stripped of decoration, remains still until the Easter Vigil, the most sacred liturgy of the year. Just as the disciples waited in sorrow and uncertainty, we, too, embrace this time of longing, knowing that darkness will soon give way to light.

Our meals on Holy Saturday remain simple, reflecting the solemnity of the day, yet they also carry a quiet expectation. In the same way we prepare our homes for Easter, we also prepare our hearts, knowing that soon the feast will come. As night falls and the Easter fire is lit, we rejoice—Christ has conquered death, and our waiting turns to glory.

As people prepare for their upcoming Easter feast and celebration, they might consider a small and friendly gathering on Saturday evening. But keep it traditional, too, as Holy Saturday is an important day in Holy Week.

STUFFED GRAPE LEAVES

Using the leaves from the grapevine plant as a food has a long history dating back to ancient times in numerous cultures—Mediterranean to the Middle East. A typical food offering has been a grape leaf filled with a mixture of meats and/or vegetables with rice and various spices or herbs.

1. Dry roast the pine nuts in a skillet until golden brown. Set aside to cool.

2. In a large, shallow saucepan with a lid, heat 4 tablespoons olive oil over medium heat. Add the diced onion and sauté for 6 minutes. Add the scallions and garlic and continue sautéing until the onions become translucent, about 4 minutes more.

3. Add the rice, and sauté for 2 minutes. Add 1 ½ cups of water and cover the saucepan with the lid. Bring to a gentle boil over medium heat and simmer the rice for about 5 minutes. All of the water should be absorbed by the rice. Remove from the heat and let cool. Transfer to a large mixing bowl.

4. While the rice is cooling, rinse the grape leaves under cold water and pat dry. Cut the stems off. Set aside torn leaves. Add the pine nuts, chopped herbs, lemon zest, spices, and capers to the cooled rice and mix well.

5. Line the used saucepan with the torn grape leaves. Spread the lemon slices on top. Place a grape leaf on a clean surface with the vein side up. Place one tablespoon of the rice filling in the center of the leaf. First fold the bottom pieces up over the filling, then fold the sides over the filling, and roll upwards. Don't roll them too tightly, as the filling will expand while cooking. Place the stuffed grape leaves in the prepared saucepan, packing them in tightly, layer after layer.

INGREDIENTS

SERVES 8 TO 10

½ cup **pine nuts**

½ cup **olive oil**

1 **onion**, peeled and diced

1 bunch **scallions**, diced

4 cloves **garlic**, peeled and minced

1 ½ cups **rice**, well rinsed

1 jar **grape leaves** in brine (40 pieces)

1 bunch fresh **dill**, rinsed and finely chopped

1 package fresh **mint leaves**, rinsed and finely chopped

1 bunch fresh **parsley**, rinsed and finely chopped

Zest and **juice** of 1 **lemon**

Salt and freshly ground **pepper**, to taste

Ground **nutmeg**, to taste

½ cup **capers**

1 large **lemon**, cut into ¼-inch slices

6. Add 1 ½ cups of water, the lemon juice, and the remaining 4 tablespoons of olive oil. Place a heavy dinner plate upside down on top of the grape leaf rolls to hold them down during cooking. Cover the saucepan with a lid. Bring to a gentle boil over medium-low heat and simmer for about 1 hour. Remove from the heat and let stand for another hour.

7. Remove them from the saucepan and transfer to a flat foil or plastic pan. Cover and then refrigerate.

These taste best if they are made a day or two in advance. Any leftover filling works well in stuffed peppers.

EASTER SEASON

Let Us Pray

℣. Queen of Heaven, rejoice, alleluia.

℟. For He whom you did merit to bear, alleluia.

℣. Has risen, as he said, alleluia.

℟. Pray for us to God, alleluia.

℣. Rejoice and be glad, O Virgin Mary, alleluia.

℟. For the Lord has truly risen, alleluia.

EASTER SEASON

The sorrow of Good Friday gives way to radiant joy on Easter morning, as the tomb stands empty and the cry resounds: He is risen! The Easter season is the heart of the Christian year, celebrating the triumph of Christ over sin and death. In the glorious light of the Resurrection, all creation rejoices, for our Redeemer lives and His victory is ours.

Easter is not a single day, but a fifty-day feast, beginning with Easter Sunday and culminating in the great celebration of Pentecost. These holy days are marked by alleluias and lilies, baptismal waters and burning candles—signs of the new life Christ won for us. From the appearances of the risen Lord to the sending of the Holy Spirit, the Church journeys with awe through the unfolding mystery of redemption fulfilled.

During this season, we remember that Christ's Resurrection is not only a past event, but a present reality and a future promise. He who once lay in the tomb now reigns at the right hand of the Father, and through Him, we are made new. The feasts of Divine Mercy, the Ascension, and Pentecost guide our hearts from the empty tomb to the outpouring of the Spirit, calling us to live as Easter people—people of hope, joy, and mission.

This is a season of renewal, community, and celebration. As we gather at table, breaking bread and sharing the fruits of the earth, may our feasting reflect the joy of the risen Christ and the communion we share in His Body. Let every dish prepared and every heart lifted in thanksgiving echo the song of the angels: Christ is risen, alleluia!

The liturgical color for Easter is white and gold. We celebrate the glorious Resurrection of Jesus Christ, and brilliant white table linens can be a way for us to dress our table for the occasion.

EASTER SUNDAY FEAST

Resurrection Rolls

Deviled Eggs

Dates Stuffed with Pistachios

Rachel's Roast Lamb

Creamy Mashed Potatoes

Fresh Asparagus with Red Peppers,
Almonds, and Olives

Easy Buttermilk Drop Biscuits

Pashka

Let Us Pray

Christ is Risen: The world below lies desolate.

Christ is Risen: The spirits of evil are fallen.

Christ is Risen: The angels of God are rejoicing.

Christ is Risen: The tombs of the dead are empty.

Christ is Risen indeed from the dead,

the first of the sleepers,

Glory and power are his forever and ever. Amen.

EASTER SUNDAY

Easter Sunday is the pinnacle of the Christian year—the day of victory, joy, and new life. After the sorrow of Good Friday and the silence of Holy Saturday, the Church bursts into celebration, proclaiming, "Christ is risen! Alleluia!" The darkness of the tomb has been overcome by the brilliance of the Resurrection, and, with it, we are given the promise of eternal life.

Fittingly, Easter is a day of feasting, a joyful contrast to the fasting and simplicity of the days before. Families and friends gather around the table to celebrate, sharing a meal that reflects the abundant joy of Christ's triumph. Traditional Easter foods—often rich and symbolic—remind us of God's providence and the new life we have in Him. Just as Jesus broke bread with His disciples after rising from the dead, we, too, break bread in thanksgiving, savoring not only the food before us but the boundless love of our risen Lord.

Easter is more than a single day—it is a season of joy that lasts fifty days. As we feast, we do so in the spirit of gratitude, knowing that through Christ's Resurrection, we are made new, and the feast of Heaven awaits us. Alleluia!

SHOPPING LIST

BAKING SUPPLIES

All-purpose flour	2 cups
Confectioners' sugar	2 cups
Sugar, granulated	½ cup

BREAD

Refrigerated crescent rolls	8–12 ounce package

CANNED GOODS

Baking powder	
Baking soda	
Crispy fried onions	
Kalamata olives	¼ cup
Maraschino cherries	½ cup

CONDIMENTS AND SAUCES

Dijon mustard	2 teaspoons
Mayonnaise	3 tablespoons
Tabasco or hot sauce	

DRY FOODS

Almonds, sliced	¾ cup
Almonds, slivered	¾ cup
Marshmallows	8 large
Medjool dates, pitted	16 dates (12 ounces)
Pistachios, whole and shelled	16 nuts

EGGS AND DAIRY

Blue cheese, crumbled	1 tablespoon
Butter, unsalted	5 sticks
Buttermilk (can substitute with 1 cup of milk mixed with 1 tablespoon of vinegar)	1 cup
Cream cheese	Four 8-ounce packages
Eggs	9 large
Feta cheese	½ cup
Heavy cream	¾ cup

MEAT

Leg of Lamb	5 pound

OIL AND VINEGAR

Olive oil	

PRODUCE

Asparagus	2 pounds
Currants	¾ cup
Garlic	1 head
Lemon	1 large
Mint, fresh	
Oregano, fresh	2 tablespoons
Parsley	1 bunch
Red bell pepper	1 medium
Russet potatoes	6 large
Strawberries	
Thyme, fresh	½ teaspoon

SPICES

Cinnamon, ground	
Vanilla extract	

RESURRECTION ROLLS

On Easter morning, Mary Magdalene—along with the other Mary—came to Jesus' tomb in order to anoint his body with burial spices, in accord with Jewish custom. Imagine her joy and astonishment upon hearing the message of God's angel, "He is not here, but has risen" (Luke 24:5). It was only three days prior that she had witnessed her Lord die on the Cross and be laid in the tomb. This recipe especially appeals to children, and it is a wonderful way of celebrating the Resurrection with your family. As you prepare this recipe, you will follow in the footsteps of Mary Magdalene: as the rolls bake, the marshmallow, wrapped in the roll and anointed with oils (butter) and spices, will "resurrect," leaving behind the empty tomb!

1. Preheat the oven to 375 degrees F. Grease a jumbo-sized muffin pan with butter and set it aside.

2. Separate the rolls into eight triangles. In a shallow dish, combine the sugar and cinnamon. Dip each marshmallow into butter, roll in the cinnamon sugar, and place it on a dough triangle. Pinch the dough around the marshmallow, sealing all edges. Make sure to seal well, or all the marshmallows will escape.

3. Dip the tops of dough into the remaining butter and cinnamon sugar. Place the pouches in the muffin tins, sugar side up. Using a jumbo-sized muffin pan keeps the juice from overflowing.

4. Bake for 10 to 14 minutes, or until the rolls are golden brown. Remove from the oven and allow to cool slightly, then eat warm.

INGREDIENTS

YIELD: 6 TO 8 ROLLS

8-ounce or 12-ounce **package refrigerated crescent rolls** (the bigger size makes it a little easier to wrap around the marshmallows)

¼ cup **granulated sugar**

1 tablespoon ground **cinnamon**

8 large **marshmallows**

¼ cup **butter**, melted

Jumbo marshmallows may not stay sealed in the dough while baking, so the best choice is using only large-sized marshmallows.

DEVILED EGGS

DON'T BE SCARED BY THE NAME—"deviled" is a culinary term originating in the
eighteenth century for a dish that has been heavily spiced or seasoned. Boiled eggs
also have a storied tradition dating back to ancient Rome. While they weren't
"deviled," seasoned boiled eggs were a common dish in Roman high society.

1. Put the eggs in a large saucepan and cover them with cool water.
   Cover the pan with a lid and bring the water to a boil over medium-high heat. Boil for about 8 minutes. Remove the eggs from the
   heat with a slotted spoon and place them in a bowl of ice water.
   When the eggs are cold, remove the eggs from the water, crack the
   shells, and peel the eggs clean.

2. Cut the eggs in half lengthwise and scoop out the yolks into a
   mixing bowl. Mash them with a fork and stir in the mayonnaise
   and Dijon mustard until smooth. Then fold in the crumbled blue
   cheese and Tabasco, if desired.

3. Spoon the mixture into each egg half. Arrange the eggs on a serving platter and garnish with the fried onion crumbles and the
   parsley.

INGREDIENTS

SERVES 6

6 large **eggs**

3 tablespoons **mayonnaise**

2 teaspoons **Dijon mustard**

1 tablespoon crumbled **blue
cheese**

Dash of **Tabasco** (optional)

Crispy fried onions, crumbled,
for garnish

Chopped **parsley**, for garnish

DATES STUFFED WITH PISTACHIOS

Dates, revered in the Torah as one of the seven species blessing ancient Israel (Deut. 8:8), symbolize prosperity and sustenance, epitomized by the land "flowing with milk and honey," often thought to refer to date honey. Their historical and poetic significance is celebrated, with the Psalmist likening the righteous to flourishing date palms (see Ps. 92:12).

1. Open the dates gently, and carefully spoon in ½ teaspoon of feta cheese.

2. Place the pistachios into each date and arrange the dates on a serving plate. Sprinkle with the parsley.

For a less Biblical but delicious variation, wrap each prepared date in a strip of bacon and roast in a 400-degree F oven until the bacon is done to your liking.

INGREDIENTS

SERVES 6 TO 8

16 **Medjool dates** (12 ounces), pitted

½ cup **feta cheese crumbles** at room temperature, or more as needed

16 whole **pistachios**, shelled

Chopped **parsley**, for garnish

16 strips **bacon**, optional (see note)

RACHEL'S ROAST LAMB

Lamb has traditionally been a staple on Easter Sunday, and for good reason. The book of Revelation paints a vivid image of the "Lamb standing, as though it had been slain" (Rev. 5:6). Because of its connection with Jewish sacrificial worship, the Lamb is a clear image of Christ: the definitive, perfect, and pure sacrifice for man's sins.

1. Make 5 slits in the leg of lamb and push the garlic cloves into the slits. Combine the oil, oregano, thyme, salt, pepper, and lemon juice in a mixing bowl. Rub the lamb with the oil mixture and put the leg onto a rack in the roasting pan. Let the meat marinate for several hours.

2. Preheat the oven to 350 degrees F. Line a roasting pan with foil and set aside. Add the lamb and roast, basting frequently, until it reaches an internal temperature of 130 to 135 degrees for medium-rare, about 1 ½ to 2 hours. Remove from the oven, cover with foil, and let it sit for 15 minutes. Serve on a platter and garnish with mint.

INGREDIENTS

SERVES 6 TO 8

5-pound **leg of lamb**

5 cloves **garlic**, peeled and gently crushed

½ cup **olive oil**

2 tablespoons crumbled fresh **oregano**

½ teaspoon fresh **thyme**

Salt and freshly ground **black pepper**, to taste

Juice of 1 **lemon**

Chopped **mint**, for garnish

LAMB DONENESS GUIDE			
Medium-Rare	Medium	Medium-Well	Well Done
130 degrees F	140 degrees F	150 degrees F	160 degrees F

CREAMY MASHED POTATOES

THIS CREAMY MASHED POTATOES RECIPE OFFERS a simple yet sublime side that mirrors the season's liturgical white, promising a comforting addition to your festive table.

1. Boil the potatoes, skin on and whole, until fork tender. Drain the potatoes completely and leave the skins on, if desired. Break the potatoes into small pieces into a large mixing bowl.

2. Using an electric mixer, start whipping the potatoes, slowly adding the butter and liquid. Do not overbeat or add too much liquid, or the potatoes will become soupy. Season to taste.

INGREDIENTS

SERVES 4 TO 6

6 baking **potatoes**

6 to 8 tablespoons **butter**, melted

¾ cup **heavy cream** or **regular milk** or **chicken stock**

Salt and freshly ground **black pepper**, to taste

FRESH ASPARAGUS WITH RED PEPPERS, ALMONDS, AND OLIVES

ALTHOUGH ASPARAGUS HAS A LONG HISTORY dating back to ancient Greece and Rome, no records suggest that the ancient Israelites grew or ate asparagus. But, we know that they did enjoy almonds and olives. Even from prehistoric times, almonds were widespread and even mentioned in the Bible as a "choice fruit" sent by Jacob to the ruler of Egypt (Gen. 43:11). And olives and olive oil were basic elements in ancient Israelite cooking and meals.

1. Heat a large skillet over medium-high heat and add the olive oil and butter. When the butter has melted, add the asparagus, laid out flat, and coat with the olive oil. Season with salt and pepper.

2. Add the diced red bell pepper and cook for 5 to 10 minutes, or until the asparagus is tender but still slightly crisp.

3. Remove from the skillet and place on a serving platter. Garnish with the almonds and olives before serving.

INGREDIENTS

SERVES 6

3 tablespoons **olive oil**

2 tablespoons **butter**

2 pounds fresh **asparagus**, ends trimmed

Salt and freshly ground **black pepper**, to taste

¾ cup diced **red bell peppers**

¾ cup **slivered almonds**

4 tablespoons **pitted kalamata olives**, slivered

EASY BUTTERMILK DROP BISCUITS

1. Preheat the oven to 425 degrees F. Line a large baking sheet with parchment paper and set aside.

2. Place the butter in a microwave-safe dish and melt it on high. Set aside.

3. In a separate large mixing bowl, whisk together the flour, baking powder, sugar, salt, and baking soda. Measure the buttermilk and whisk it into the melted butter with a fork. Stir until the mixture looks lumpy, about 1 minute.

4. Pour the buttermilk mixture into the dry ingredients and stir it together with a spatula. Don't overmix the dough—stop as soon as all the flour has just been incorporated, scraping the sides of the bowl as you go.

5. Use a large tablespoon to scoop up 12 even balls of dough and drop them on the prepared baking sheet in 4 rows of 3. Gently pat the edges of the dough down so that the biscuits will brown evenly.

6. Bake the biscuits for 13 to 15 minutes or until golden brown underneath and just starting to brown on top. Melt the remaining 2 tablespoons of butter and use a pastry brush to paint the tops of the biscuits while they are still warm. Serve immediately.

INGREDIENTS

MAKES 12 BISCUITS

8 tablespoons (1 stick) **butter**

2 cups **all-purpose flour**

2 teaspoons **baking powder**

1 teaspoon **granulated sugar**

½ teaspoon **salt**

½ teaspoon **baking soda**

1 cup cold **buttermilk**, or more as needed (see note)

2 tablespoons **butter**, for brushing on top of baked biscuits

If you cannot find buttermilk, you can make your own by mixing 1 cup of whole milk with 1 tablespoon of vinegar and letting it sit for 10 minutes.

PASHKA

THIS EASTERN ORTHODOX DESSERT—NAMED after the Slavic word for Easter, *Pashka*—is a traditional Easter treat that is similar in texture to a rich cheesecake. It is formed in a flowerpot lined with moist cheesecloth, making it symbolic of the tomb of Jesus. Traditionally, an "XB" is marked on the top, which is the abbreviation for "Christ is Risen" in some eastern European languages.

1. Line a moistened 8- to 10-inch flowerpot or a 2-quart flowerpot with doubled cheesecloth. Set aside.

2. Blend together the cream cheese and the butter until smooth. Add the eggs, sugar, and vanilla extract, and fold in the almonds, currants, and maraschino cherries. Pour in the mixture, cover with plastic wrap, and refrigerate for 48 hours.

3. Before serving, pull the pashka from the flowerpot using the cheesecloth and peel the cheesecloth off. Serve with the strawberries as garnish.

This should be prepared 48 hours before serving so that it firms in the refrigerator. The flowerpot must be moistened beforehand and lined with cheesecloth before adding the filling.

INGREDIENTS

SERVES 6 TO 8

Four 8-ounce packages **cream cheese**, at room temperature

1 cup **butter**, at room temperature

3 **egg yolks**

2 cups **confectioners' sugar**

3 tablespoons **vanilla extract**

¾ cup **sliced almonds**

¾ cup **currants**

½ cup diced **maraschino cherries**

Whole strawberries

DIVINE MERCY SUNDAY

Second Sunday of Easter

Celebrated on the first Sunday after Easter, Divine Mercy Sunday is a feast rooted in the profound love and mercy of God. Instituted by Pope St. John Paul II in the year 2000, this feast is inspired by the visions of St. Faustina Kowalska, a Polish nun who recorded Jesus' messages of mercy in her diary. The devotion of praying the Divine Mercy Chaplet can be traced back to St. Faustina's visions.

On this day, Catholics are encouraged to reflect on God's endless compassion, receive the Sacrament of Reconciliation, and pray the Divine Mercy Chaplet. The imagery of Christ's Divine Mercy — red and white rays flowing from His heart — symbolizes the blood and water that poured from His side on the Cross, representing His love and salvation.

DIVINE MERCY SHORTCAKE

THIS DIVINE MERCY SHORTCAKE IS INSPIRED by the Divine Mercy image, which shows the blood and water that gushed forth from Christ's side at the Crucifixion as rays of light emanating from Jesus' heart. The cake itself is pieced together in the shape of a heart, and the rays of blood and water are represented here by the macerated strawberries and whipped cream.

AS THE RECIPE DONOR NOTES, "THIS makes a lot of cake, but if you're not serving a crowd, break up the leftover cake in a bowl, top with leftover strawberries and juices, and leftover whipped cream, and you have trifle for dessert the next day!"

1. Preheat the oven to 375 degrees F. Grease and parchment line an 8-inch square and an 8-inch round cake pan and set aside.

2. In the bowl of a food processor or in a large mixing bowl, add the flour, sugar, baking powder, and salt. Add the butter bits and pulse until the butter and flour resemble coarse crumbs—it should come together fairly quickly. If making by hand, cut the butter in with a pastry cutter. Add the milk and eggs and pulse just a few times, just until the dry ingredients are moistened, or use a spatula and mix just until the dry ingredients are moistened. Divide the mixture between the two pans and smooth with a spatula. Sprinkle with a few teaspoons of granulated sugar.

3. Bake for 25 to 30 minutes until a toothpick comes out clean. Let cool for 20 minutes.

4. Meanwhile, place the strawberries in a bowl and sprinkle with sugar. Let them sit at room temperature until the berries are juicy. Chill until ready to serve.

INGREDIENTS

SERVES 10 TO 12

SHORTCAKE

4 cups **all-purpose flour**

1 cup **granulated sugar**

2 tablespoons **baking powder**

1 teaspoon **salt**

1 cup **unsalted butter**, cut in small pieces

1 ½ cups **milk**

4 **eggs**

Confectioners' sugar, for sprinkling

FRUIT

1 ½ pounds **strawberries**, hulled, cleaned, and diced

1 cup **granulated sugar**

5. After 20 minutes, remove cakes from the pans. Place the square cake on a serving platter and rotate it 45 degrees so that the point is against the edge of the plate (it should look like a diamond). Cut the round cake in half crosswise (forming two semicircles) and place each of the two halves, right side up, against the opposite sides of the square to form the shape of a heart. Cool completely. Sprinkle with confectioners' sugar.

6. Whip the cream, confectioners' sugar, and one drop of blue food coloring (if desired) at high speed until peaks form—don't overbeat.

7. Spoon half the cream on the right seam between the round and the square. Spoon half the strawberries on the left seam. Reserve extra berries and cream for serving the entire cake.

CREAM

2 cups **whipping cream**

1/2 cup **confectioners' sugar**

1 drop **blue food color** (optional)

Let Us Pray

Only begotten Son of God, having conquered death, Thou didst pass from earth to Heaven! As Son of Man seated in great glory on Thy throne and praised by the whole angelic host, grant that we who in the jubilant devotion of our faith, celebrate Thine Ascension to the Father, may not be fettered by the chains of sin to earthly loves. And may the aim of our unceasing prayer be directed toward the heavens whither, after Thy Passion, Thou didst ascend in glory.

SOLEMNITY OF THE ASCENSION OF THE LORD

—Holy Day of Obligation —

FORTY DAYS AFTER EASTER

Celebrated forty days after Easter Sunday, the Feast of the Ascension commemorates the resurrected Christ's return to Heaven, as recorded in Mark 16:19, Luke 24:51, and Acts 1:2. After His Resurrection, Jesus remained on earth for forty days, appearing to His disciples, strengthening their faith, and preparing them to spread the gospel.

According to Acts 1:1–11, before ascending, Christ instructed His apostles to remain in Jerusalem and wait for the Holy Spirit, which would empower them to become His witnesses "to the end of the earth" (Acts 1:8) Then, before their eyes, He was lifted into Heaven, disappearing into a cloud.

The Ascension marks the completion of Christ's earthly mission and the beginning of the apostles' mission to spread the Faith. It also reminds us of His promise to send the Holy Spirit, which was fulfilled at Pentecost. This solemn feast is a time of joy and hope, calling us to live out our Faith and look forward to Christ's glorious return.

CHICKEN SALAD SANDWICH

IN SOME PLACES, IT IS A tradition to serve a poultry or bird meal this day because tradition says that Jesus flew to Heaven. Keeping that in mind, some countries serve quail or duck on this feast day, but a chicken salad sandwich—even though chickens don't actually fly—makes a perfect lunch or dinner dish.

1. In a large bowl, whisk the mustard, mayonnaise, and olive oil together. Stir in the diced red onion, the chopped parsley, the parmesan cheese, and the garlic powder, combining well. Fold in the diced chicken and chopped cashews.

2. To serve, open the croissants or hamburger rolls and spoon in the salad mixture.

INGREDIENTS

SERVES 4

¼ cup **yellow mustard**

2 tablespoons **mayonnaise**, or more as needed

2 teaspoons **olive oil**

3 tablespoons diced **red onion**

3 tablespoons chopped **parsley**

2 ½ tablespoons grated **parmesan cheese**

½ teaspoon **garlic powder**

1 ½ cups diced grilled or baked **chicken breast**

12 chopped **cashews**

4 **croissants** or large **hamburger rolls**

Let Us Pray

Spirit of Christ, stir me; Spirit of Christ, move me; Spirit of Christ, fill me; Spirit of Christ, seal me. Consecrate in me Your Heart and Will, O Heavenly Father. Create in me a fountain of virtues. Seal my soul as Your own, that Your reflection in me may be a light for all to see. Amen.

SOLEMNITY OF PENTECOST

FIFTY DAYS AFTER EASTER

Pentecost, also known as Whitsunday, marks the powerful moment when the Holy Spirit descended upon the Blessed Virgin Mary and the apostles, as recorded in the Acts of the Apostles 2:1–4. Fifty days after Easter, this great solemnity celebrates the birth of the Church, when the disciples, once fearful, were filled with divine fire and sent forth to proclaim the Gospel in many tongues.

But Pentecost is not just a Christian celebration—it has deep roots in ancient Jewish tradition. Long before the events of Acts 2, the Israelites observed this day as the Feast of Weeks, also called the Feast of Harvest (see Exod. 23, Num. 28, Deut. 16). It was a joyous time of thanksgiving for the first fruits of the wheat harvest, when God's people gathered to offer the best of their labors in gratitude. The connection is profound: just as Pentecost in the Old Testament celebrated an abundant harvest, the Christian Pentecost marks the spiritual harvest of souls brought into the Church through the Holy Spirit's outpouring.

As we gather around the table, let us remember: the same Holy Spirit who ignited the hearts of the apostles continues to move in our lives today, filling us with grace, courage, and the fire of divine love.

PENTECOST CAKE

A CHEERFUL WAY TO CELEBRATE THE day is to gather for prayers with others and to serve a tempting lunch or dinner, concluding with a luscious birthday cake. After all, Pentecost honors the descent of the Holy Spirit, which is why it's often called the birthday of the Church.

1. Preheat the oven to 350 degrees F.

2. Scald the milk and allow it to cool. Sift the sugar, flour, and baking powder together three times. Add the scalded milk gradually, beating constantly.

3. Add the egg whites to a mixing bowl along with the cream of tartar, salt, and vanilla. Beat for 1 ½ to 2 minutes, or until the egg whites don't slip when the bowl is tipped. Fold the whites into the batter.

4. Bake in an ungreased 7-inch tube pan for 45 minutes or until the cake is golden brown and firm to the touch. Invert the cake on a rack until cool.

5. Meanwhile, hull and clean 15 large strawberries. Crush 8 of them with a fork and sweeten to taste.

6. Place the butter and confectioners' sugar into a bowl and add about 1 ½ tablespoons of the crushed berries and juice, beating well with a fork. Add only enough berries and juice to make a frosting that will spread easily. Frost the cake and top it with seven whole strawberries—symbolizing the gifts of the Holy Spirit.

INGREDIENTS

SERVES 4 TO 6

⅔ cup **milk**, scalded and cooled

1 cup **granulated sugar**

1 ⅓ cups **all-purpose flour**, sifted

1 tablespoon **baking powder**

2 **egg whites**

1 teaspoon **vanilla extract**

½ teaspoon **cream of tartar**

½ teaspoon **salt**

FROSTING

15 large **strawberries**, hulled and cleaned

1 ½ cups **confectioners' sugar**

2 tablespoons **butter**, at room temperature

Sugar, to taste

Ordinary Time
Between Pentecost and Advent

Feast Day Recipes

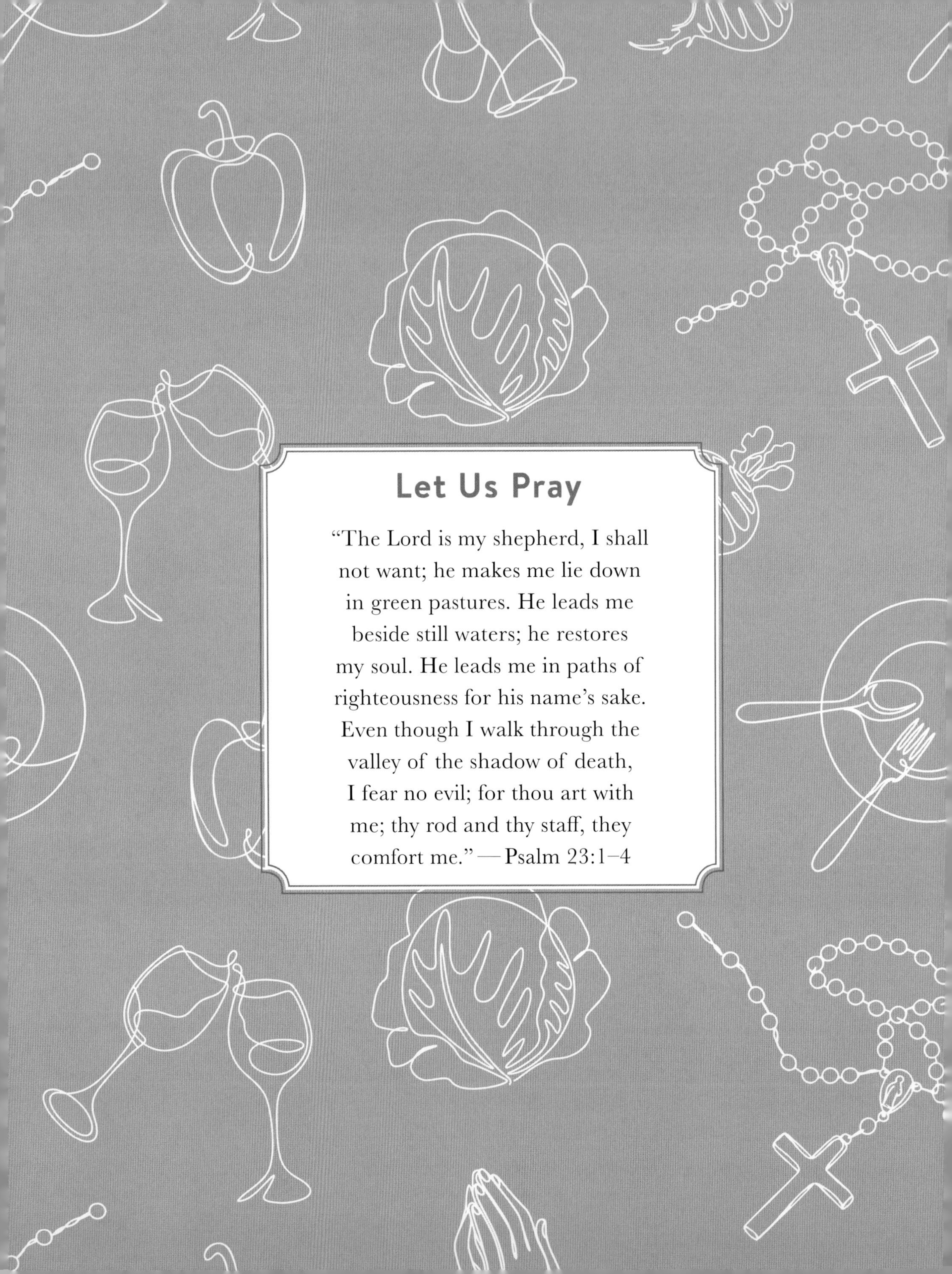

Let Us Pray

"The Lord is my shepherd, I shall not want; he makes me lie down in green pastures. He leads me beside still waters; he restores my soul. He leads me in paths of righteousness for his name's sake. Even though I walk through the valley of the shadow of death, I fear no evil; for thou art with me; thy rod and thy staff, they comfort me." — Psalm 23:1–4

ORDINARY TIME: BETWEEN PENTECOST AND ADVENT

Ordinary Time is not called "ordinary" because it is uninteresting or common. Rather, the name comes from the Latin word *ordo*, which is where we get the English word "order." In other words, Ordinary Time reflects the order of the Church year.

Unlike the celebratory feasts of Easter or Pentecost, Ordinary Time reminds us that holiness is found in the daily, in the simple joys of gathering with loved ones, breaking bread, and nourishing both body and soul. It reflects the beauty of the mundane, where God's grace is woven into the routines of cooking, sharing, and savoring the gifts He provides.

As we journey through this season, may our kitchens become places of grace, where simple meals are transformed into acts of love, and where we remember that even in the quietest seasons, Christ is with us.

Let Us Pray

Glory be to the Father,
who by His almighty power and love created me,
making me in the image and likeness of God.

Glory be to the Son,
who by His Precious Blood delivered me from Hell,
and opened for me the gates of Heaven.

Glory be to the Holy Spirit,
who has sanctified me in the sacrament of Baptism,
and continues to sanctify me.

Amen.

SOLEMNITY OF THE MOST HOLY TRINITY

FIRST SUNDAY AFTER PENTECOST

One week after Pentecost, the Church turns her heart to the greatest mystery of our Faith—the Holy Trinity. Trinity Sunday, also called the Solemnity of the Most Holy Trinity, is a moveable feast, shifting each year with the date of Easter, yet always reminding us of the eternal truth: God is three Persons—Father, Son, and Holy Spirit—yet One God.

This feast, formally established in the fourteenth century, is more than a day on the liturgical calendar; it is a joyful "Te Deum" of gratitude for the blessings of Christmas, Easter, and Pentecost. In the Trinity, we see the fullness of God's love: the Father who created us, the Son who redeemed us, and the Holy Spirit who sanctifies us. Every Baptism, every blessing, every prayer is made in the name of the Father, and of the Son, and of the Holy Spirit.

As we celebrate this solemnity, we are reminded that every Sunday is a day of devotion to the Holy Trinity. May this feast deepen our awe and love for the triune God, who calls us into His divine life and remains with us always.

GOD CAKES

In England, these have traditionally been made to celebrate New Year's Day. But as the recipe source notes, "The triangle shape is a reminder of the Trinity, which would make them also appropriate for Trinity Sunday."

1. Preheat the oven to 450 degrees F.

2. In a medium-sized glass or stainless steel bowl, mix the butter and sugar thoroughly and add the currants, lemon peel, and spices. Heat in a double boiler for a few minutes, then allow the filling to cool before using.

3. Roll out the puff pastry or pie dough ¼-inch thick and cut into 3-inch squares. Place a teaspoon of filling in one corner of each square. Moisten the edges of the pastry and fold over from corner to corner to make a triangle. Seal the edges with a fork. Place the triangles on a baking sheet.

4. Bake at 450 degrees F for 10 minutes. Reduce the heat to 350 degrees F and bake for an additional 10 minutes, or until golden brown. Remove from the oven and serve.

INGREDIENTS

SERVES 4 TO 6

¼ cup **butter**

¼ cup **granulated sugar**

¾ cup **currants**

⅓ cup **lemon peel**

½ teaspoon ground **nutmeg**

¼ teaspoon **allspice**

Puffy pastry or **pie dough**

CROWNING OF MARY

Sunday in May

The May Crowning is a beloved Catholic tradition that honors the Blessed Virgin Mary as Queen of Heaven. Dating back to the eighth century, the practice of crowning sacred images of Mary was first recorded when Pope Gregory III (731–741) donated a golden diadem to a holy image at St. Peter's Basilica. Over time, this devotion merged with the tradition of Marian devotion in May, solidifying the month as a time to venerate Our Lady.

Though there is no set date for May Crowning, many parishes hold ceremonies on Mother's Day or at the beginning of the month. In 2018, Pope Francis added a Marian feast to the liturgical calendar: Mary, Mother of the Church, celebrated the day after Pentecost. May is also rich with Marian feast days, including Our Lady of Fatima (May 13), Mary Help of Christians (May 24), and the Visitation (May 31).

The May Crowning ceremony often takes place during Mass and includes a procession, hymns, and prayers. A floral crown is placed upon Mary's statue, symbolizing her role as our heavenly Queen and Mother. This tradition invites the faithful to renew their devotion to Mary and seek her intercession throughout the month.

CINNAMON CROWN CAKE

THIS CAKE IS BAKED IN A Bundt pan to mirror the regal form of a crown. Infused with warm cinnamon and sweet applesauce, this regal cake mirrors the spirit of veneration and joy appropriate to the day.

1. Preheat the oven to 325 degrees F. Generously grease a 12-cup Bundt pan, lightly sprinkle with flour, and set aside.

2. Whisk together the flour, baking powder, and salt. Set aside. Using an electric mixer on medium speed, beat the sugar and butter until light. Add the milk, eggs, and vanilla extract, and mix well.

3. Reduce mixer speed to low. Gradually add the flour mixture, mixing just until combined. Spoon half of the batter into the prepared pan. Stir the remaining ingredients into the remaining batter. Spoon this mixture over the batter in the pan without mixing the two batters.

4. Bake for 1 hour to 1 hour 10 minutes, or until a metal skewer inserted into the center comes out clean. Cool the cake in the pan on a wire rack for 30 minutes. Then invert the cake onto a serving plate before slicing and serving.

INGREDIENTS

SERVES 12 TO 16

3 cups **all-purpose flour**, plus extra for sprinkling

1 tablespoon **baking powder**

½ teaspoon **salt**

2 cups **granulated sugar**

1 cup **unsalted butter**, softened

1 cup **milk**

3 large **eggs**

1 tablespoon **vanilla extract**

½ cup chopped **pecans**

½ cup **quick-cooking oats**

½ cup firmly packed **brown sugar**

½ cup **applesauce**

2 teaspoons ground **cinnamon**

MAY 13

OUR LADY OF FATIMA

— Fatima —

During the turmoil of World War I, Our Lady of Fatima appeared six times to three shepherd children — Lucia, Francisco, and Jacinta — in Fatima, Portugal, between May 13 and October 13, 1917. She urged them to pray the Rosary daily for peace and the conversion of sinners. She also foretold that Francisco and Jacinta would soon enter Heaven, while Lucia would remain to spread her message.

On October 13, 1917, before seventy thousand witnesses, the Miracle of the Sun occurred — the sun whirling and zigzagging in the sky — confirming the authenticity of the apparitions. Our Lady revealed herself as the Lady of the Rosary and shared three prophetic secrets, including visions of Hell, the call for devotion to Mary, and predictions of World War II and Christian persecution.

Our Lady's message remains vital: prayer, penance, and trust in God. May this feast remind us to seek peace through faith and devotion to the Immaculate Heart of Mary.

CARNE VINHA D'ALHOS

THIS TRADITIONAL PORTUGUESE MARINATED PORK DISH is a perfect way to honor
Our Lady of Fatima and the rich culinary heritage of Portugal.

1. Combine the water, vinegar, and wine in a leak-proof, nonreactive container. Add the cumin, allspice, cinnamon, cloves, nutmeg, salt and pepper, and as much crushed garlic as you'd like. Mix the liquid well and add the meat. Allow the meat to marinate in the refrigerator for 2 days. This is optimal but could be shortened in a pinch.

2. Heat the oven to 375 degrees F. Place the pork in a nonreactive baking dish along with ½ cup of the marinade. Roast the meat until cooked through. The time will vary by quantity of meat. For one-inch pork chops, roast 20 to 25 minutes, or until the meat reaches an internal temperature of 145 degrees F. Ribs will need at least 2 hours to roast. Pour off the drippings and grease at least once during cooking. The finished meat should be without liquid, but not dry. For larger quantities of meat, increase the water, vinegar, and spices.

INGREDIENTS

SERVES 4 TO 6

2 cups **water**

1 cup **apple cider** or **red wine vinegar**

1 cup **white wine**

Lots of crushed **garlic**, to taste

1 teaspoon ground **cumin**

1 teaspoon ground **allspice**

1/2 teaspoon ground **cinnamon**

1/2 teaspoon ground **cloves**

1/2 teaspoon ground **nutmeg**

Salt and freshly ground **black pepper**, to taste

2 1/2 pounds **country-style pork ribs** (more meat from boneless) or **lean pork chops**

MAY 30

ST. JOAN OF ARC

— France —

Born: 1412, Died: 1431

Born around 1412, Joan of Arc was a French peasant girl whose life changed at the age of thirteen when St. Michael, St. Margaret, and St. Catherine of Alexandria appeared to her, calling her to lead France to victory against English rule.

At just seventeen years old, she rallied French troops, leading them to a miraculous victory at Orléans on May 8, 1429. She continued to aid France until her capture on May 23, 1430. Accused of heresy and cross-dressing, she was put on trial by the English in Rouen and burned at the stake on May 30, 1431. In her final moments, she clutched a cross, embracing the Faith even in death.

Canonized in 1920, St. Joan of Arc is the patroness of France and soldiers. Her unwavering bravery and devotion to God continue to inspire the faithful today.

CRÈME BRÛLÉE

HISTORIANS NOTE THAT THIS FAMOUS FRENCH dessert was first served to French royalty, possibly in the 1600s. Today, people dispute its source. Nevertheless, it is a stunningly rich treat and an ideal dessert for this French saint.

1. Preheat the oven to 375 degrees F. Begin boiling a kettle of water for the water bath.

2. Beat the egg yolks, granulated sugar, and vanilla extract in a mixing bowl until thick and creamy. Pour the cream into a saucepan and stir over low heat until it almost comes to a boil. Remove the cream from the heat immediately. Slowly but continuously whisk the warmed cream into the egg yolk mixture until combined.

3. Pour the mixture evenly into six individual 6-ounce ramekins. Place the ramekins in a large heatproof baking dish and pour hot water into the dish until it reaches halfway up the sides of the ramekins. Be careful to not get water into the ramekins.

4. Bake on the middle rack of the preheated oven for 15 to 20 minutes. The custard should jiggle just slightly in the middle. Remove from the oven and let it cool in the water bath for about 15 minutes, then remove and chill in the refrigerator for 2 to 3 hours.

5. When ready to serve, position your oven rack so that the top of the ramekins will be 3 to 4 inches below the broiler and preheat your broiler to high. Evenly sprinkle the top of each ramekin with turbinado sugar. Place the ramekins on a rimmed baking sheet and broil until the sugar browns, 2 to 5 minutes. Be sure to keep an eye on them, as the sugar browns very quickly. Serve immediately.

INGREDIENTS

SERVES 4 TO 6

6 **egg yolks**

4 tablespoons **granulated sugar**

½ teaspoon **vanilla extract**

2 ½ cups **heavy cream**

2 tablespoons **turbinado sugar**

If you cannot find turbinado sugar, you can substitute it with brown sugar.

Let Us Pray

Lord Jesus Christ, we worship You living among us in the sacrament of your Body and Blood. May we offer to our Father in Heaven a solemn pledge of undivided love. May we offer to our brothers and sisters a life poured out in loving service of that kingdom where You live with the Father and the Holy Spirit, one God for ever and ever. Amen.

SOLEMNITY OF CORPUS CHRISTI, THE MOST HOLY BODY AND BLOOD OF CHRIST

LATE MAY OR MID-JUNE

Corpus Christi, Latin for "Body of Christ," is a solemn feast celebrating the Real Presence of Jesus in the Holy Eucharist—Body, Blood, Soul, and Divinity. Traditionally observed on the Thursday after Trinity Sunday, it honors the great mystery of the Last Supper, when Christ instituted the Eucharist. The feast is often moved from Thursday to the following Sunday.

The origins of Corpus Christi trace back to the thirteenth century, when a Eucharistic miracle occurred in Germany. A priest, struggling with doubts about the Real Presence, witnessed blood seeping from the consecrated Host during Mass. Pope Urban IV confirmed the miracle and enshrined the relics in the Cathedral of Orvieto, where they remain today. Inspired by this event and the visions of St. Juliana of Liege, Pope Urban IV established Corpus Christi as a universal feast in 1264.

At every Mass, through the miracle of transubstantiation, bread and wine become the true Body and Blood of Christ. Corpus Christi reminds us of this sacred gift and invites us to deepen our love for the Eucharist, the source and summit of our Faith.

ITALIAN PIZZELLE COOKIES

1. In a medium mixing bowl, whisk together the eggs, sugar, butter, vanilla, and baking powder until well combined. Add in the flour and mix just until the mixture is well incorporated. Let the batter sit for 30 minutes at room temperature before using.

2. Heat the pizzelle maker or waffle maker according to the manufacturer's instructions. If needed, brush the hot pizzelle iron with oil (this is not necessary for nonstick irons). Scoop about 2 teaspoons of batter onto the center of the pizzelle maker. Close the lid and cook for 30 to 60 seconds, or until the pizzelle is a light golden color. Carefully remove using tongs or a fork. Place the cooked pizzelle on a wire rack and dust with confectioners' sugar once cooled.

The pizzelle maker or iron is available online. Otherwise, you can use a waffle maker.

INGREDIENTS

YIELD: 30 COOKIES

3 large **eggs**

¾ cup **granulated sugar**

½ cup **butter**, melted and cooled

2 teaspoons **vanilla extract**

2 teaspoons **baking powder**

1 ½ cups **all-purpose flour**

Confectioners' sugar, for dusting

Let Us Pray

O most holy Heart of Jesus, fountain of every blessing, I adore You, I love You, and with lively sorrow for my sins I offer You this poor heart of mine. Make me humble, patient, pure, and wholly obedient to Your will. Grant, Good Jesus, that I may live in You and for You. Protect me in the midst of danger. Comfort me in my afflictions. Give me health of body, assistance in my temporal needs, Your blessing on all that I do, and the grace of a holy death. Amen.

SOLEMNITY OF THE MOST SACRED HEART OF JESUS

FRIDAY AFTER CORPUS CHRISTI

The Solemnity of the Sacred Heart of Jesus is celebrated on the Friday after Corpus Christi, typically falling in June. The modern devotion to the Sacred Heart began in 1673, when St. Margaret Mary Alacoque, a Visitation nun in France, received visions of Jesus over the course of eighteen months. Christ revealed His Sacred Heart to her, instructing her to promote devotion through the Holy Hour on Thursdays, the establishment of this feast, and the First Friday devotion, encouraging monthly Eucharistic reception in His honor.

In 1856, Pope Pius IX designated the feast of the Sacred Heart as a universal feast in the Church. Not long after, Pope Leo XIII consecrated the entire world to the Sacred Heart of Jesus in the encyclical *Annum Sacrum* in 1899.

This feast has not lost any of its significance since its promulgation in the nineteenth century. As John Paul II said, this feast "reminds us of the mystery of divine Love for people of every age."

PISTACHIO ROSEWATER COOKIES

Roses have long been used as symbols of love and devotion. The use of rosewater in these cookies aligns beautifully with this feast commemorating Christ's unending love and mercy to humanity.

1. In a food processor, add the flour, pistachios, confectioners' sugar, and salt. Pulse a few times until well blended. Add the butter, one cube at a time, and pulse to combine. Then add the rosewater, water, and vanilla extract. Blend until the mixture begins to form a ball.

2. Remove the dough from the food processor and place it on a lightly floured surface. Bring together into a large ball. Cut the ball into two equal parts. Roll out each part into a 9-inch-long log. Wrap the logs with plastic wrap and refrigerate for about 3 hours.

3. Preheat the oven to 325 degrees F. Line the baking sheet with parchment paper and set aside.

4. Remove the dough from the refrigerator and place each piece on a floured surface. Cut each cookie into a ½-inch circle and place on the baking sheet.

5. Bake for 12 to 14 minutes, or until they appear golden brown on the edges. Remove from the oven. When cool, sprinkle with confectioners' sugar.

INGREDIENTS

MAKES ABOUT 30 COOKIES

1 ¾ cups **all-purpose flour**

½ cup unsalted shelled **pistachios**, roasted

½ cup **confectioners' sugar**, plus extra for sprinkling

½ teaspoon **salt**

6 ounces **unsalted butter**, preferably European-style, cut in cubes

1 ½ tablespoons **rosewater**

1 tablespoon **water**

2 teaspoons **vanilla extract**

JUNE 24

ST. JOHN THE BAPTIST

— Israel —

Born: circa 5 B.C., Died: circa A.D. 31

St. John the Baptist, born just months before Christ, was divinely named — the Archangel Gabriel appeared to Zechariah, as he did for Our Lady (see Luke 1:13). His name means "God is gracious." He lived an austere life in the desert, clothed in camel's hair and sustained by locusts and wild honey (see Matt. 3:4)

As the Baptist, he called people to repentance, preparing the way for Jesus. His most profound act was baptizing Christ in the Jordan River, marking the beginning of Jesus' public ministry (see Matt. 3:13–17; Mark 1:9–11; Luke 3:21–22; cf. John 1:29–34). His fiery preaching and fearless truth-telling led to his martyrdom — he was beheaded at the request of Herodias's daughter (see Matt. 14:1–12).

He is honored as the patron saint of many places, including Jordan, Puerto Rico, Florence, and his feast day, June 24, is a joyous celebration. His life reminds us to prepare our hearts for Christ and live with unwavering faith.

HONEY CAKE

In St. Mark's Gospel (Mark 1:6), readers learn that John the Baptist during his preaching days clothed himself in camel's hair and ate locusts and honey. Certainly, then, to commemorate St. John the Baptist, the ideal treat is a honey cake.

1. Preheat the oven to 350 degrees F. Line a 9-inch round cake pan with parchment, grease with cooking spray, and set aside.

2. In a large bowl, beat the honey and butter together until the butter is smooth and the mixture is light and creamy. Add the eggs, one at a time, beating well after each addition, then add the almond extract.

3. In a separate medium bowl, whisk together the flour, salt, and baking soda. Add the dry ingredients to the honey mixture and beat until just barely combined. Then add the yogurt and beat until just combined. Pour the batter into the prepared cake pan.

4. Bake until a toothpick inserted in the middle comes out clean, 40 to 45 minutes. Remove from the oven and allow to rest for 10 minutes in the pan, then turn out on to a cooling rack and let the cake cool completely. Before serving, dust the cake with confectioners' sugar. Top with fruit, if desired.

INGREDIENTS

SERVES 6 TO 8

1 cup **honey**

½ cup (1 stick) **butter**, softened

3 **eggs**

¼ teaspoon **almond extract**

2 cups **all-purpose flour**

½ teaspoon **salt**

½ teaspoon **baking soda**

½ cup **vanilla Greek yogurt**

Confectioners' sugar, for serving

Assorted fruit, for serving

JUNE 26

ST. JOSEMARÍA ESCRIVÁ

— Spain —

Born: 1902, Died: 1974

Born in Barbastro, Spain, on January 9, 1902, St. Josemaría Escrivá de Balaguer dedicated his life to spreading holiness in everyday work. Ordained in 1925, he moved to Madrid in 1927, where he ministered to the poor and sick while studying law. On October 2, 1928, he received divine inspiration to found Opus Dei ("Work of God"), a movement calling all people — students, workers, and professionals — to seek holiness in their daily lives.

His mission extended beyond Opus Dei; in 1943, he founded the Priestly Society of the Holy Cross to support diocesan priests. His writings, especially *The Way*, have inspired millions. After his passing in 1975, he was canonized by Pope John Paul II in 2002.

St. Josemaría's message remains a powerful reminder that every task, no matter how small, can be offered to God. His feast day, June 26, is a celebration of faith lived through work and service.

CRESPILLOS

ACCORDING TO THE RECIPE DONOR, "EVERY year on the 'Friday of Sorrows' (the Friday before Palm Sunday), the mother of St. Josemaría, Dolores Escrivá, used to prepare a special dessert called "crespillos." It was a simple dessert that she would only make on that day, and thus the family always looked forward to it.... The recipe is easy to follow and inexpensive, and it makes for a tasty and original dessert for your family."

1. Wash the spinach very well and leave just 1 inch of stalk on each. Mix the flour and sugar in a bowl. Beat the eggs and milk together and then add them to the flour in increments, whisking continuously until a smooth batter forms.

2. Heat a pan of oil to 350 degrees F. Dry the spinach leaves well and coat them on both sides with the batter. Fry the leaves, several at a time, until a light golden brown. Once done, drain them on a cooling rack or paper towels. Coat each crespillo with granulated sugar and serve immediately.

INGREDIENTS

SERVES 3 TO 4

1 pound fresh **spinach leaves**

1 ⅔ cups **self-rising flour**

3 teaspoons **granulated sugar**

2 large **eggs**

½ cup plus 2 tablespoons **milk**

Oil, for frying

Sugar, for sprinkling

If you don't have self-rising flour, you can make your own by combining 1 ⅔ cup all-purpose flour, 2 ½ teaspoons of baking powder, and ¼ teaspoon salt.

JUNE 29

STS. PETER AND PAUL

— St. Peter: Israel —
— St. Paul: Tarsus —

St. Peter Born: circa 1, Died: circa 64
St. Paul Born: circa 5, Died: circa 64

The Solemnity of Sts. Peter and Paul is celebrated on June 29.

St. Peter, originally Simon, was a fisherman from Galilee when he was called by Christ to become a fisher of men. Jesus renamed him Peter, or Cephas, meaning "rock," and entrusted him with the keys to the Kingdom of Heaven. He became the Church's first pope, preaching in Jerusalem before journeying to Rome, where he was crucified under Emperor Nero and, as tradition holds, humbly requested to be crucified upside down. His tomb lies beneath St. Peter's Basilica.

St. Paul, also Saul, was a fierce persecutor of Christians until his dramatic conversion on the road to Damascus. Following his conversion and Baptism, he became the Church's greatest missionary, spreading the gospel across the Roman world. Arrested and tried under Nero, he was beheaded in Rome.

St. Peter is the patron of Rome and fishermen, while St. Paul is the patron of missionaries and writers. Their feast reminds us of their unwavering faith and their sacrifice in building Christ's Church.

FILLET OF FLOUNDER IN TOMATO SAUCE

In several English seacoast villages, St. Peter is considered the fishermen's chief protector, so his annual feast day becomes a festival. Boat owners cover their boats with ribbons and flowers and may even repaint the boat to honor St. Peter. All the townspeople gather together to observe boat races and enjoy the main dish: fish.

1. Add the onion, green bell pepper, and butter into a large saucepan and cook over medium heat until soft. Add the tomatoes to the onion and pepper and cook over low heat for about 10 minutes.

2. Stir the cream and corn starch together, add to the vegetables, and cook for a few more minutes. Bring the mixture to a boil.

3. Place the fish skin-side down on top of the vegetables, cover the pan with a lid, and cook for about 10 minutes, or until the fish is a solid white.

4. Serve covered with the vegetable sauce. Top with chopped parsley and lemon juice, to taste.

INGREDIENTS

SERVES 4 TO 6

1 **onion**, peeled and minced

1 **green bell pepper**, seeded and minced

2 to 3 tablespoons **butter**

6 **plum tomatoes**, chopped

3 tablespoons **cream**

1 tablespoon **cornstarch**

4 **flounder fillets**, skin-on.

Salt and freshly **ground black pepper**, to taste

Freshly squeezed **lemon juice**, to taste

Chopped fresh **parsley**, for garnish

JULY 3

ST. THOMAS THE APOSTLE

— Israel —

Born: Early first century,
Died: Late first century

St. Thomas, one of the twelve apostles, is best remembered for his moment of doubt after Christ's Resurrection. When the other apostles proclaimed they had seen the risen Lord, Thomas refused to believe until he touched Christ's wounds. When Jesus appeared again and invited him to do so, Thomas proclaimed, "My Lord and my God!" (John 20:28)—an act of faith that inspires believers to this day.

A dedicated disciple, Thomas bravely encouraged the apostles to follow Jesus into dangerous territory. Tradition tells us he preached the gospel in Persia and India, where he is still venerated as the founder of the Christian community. He was martyred, and his relics are kept in India, Italy, and Greece.

St. Thomas is honored as the patron saint of builders, architects, and those who struggle with doubt. His journey from doubt to unwavering belief is a powerful testament to God's grace.

GOAN RICE PULAO

As its history confirms, Goa has been a blend of cultures and cuisines, and its recipes are really delicious. For example, this rice recipe was created by a Goan native, Joe Fernandes, who cooks great Goan food and taught a Goan cooking class at his former Catholic parish in Chantilly, VA.

1. Soak the rice in cold water for 15 minutes. While the rice is soaking, in a large pot over medium-high heat, sauté the diced onion. Once golden brown, add and sauté the diced plum tomato until soft.

2. Add 3 ¾ cups water, the chicken bouillon cubes, and the spices, and bring to a boil.

3. Drain the rice completely and add it to the pot along with the peas.

4. Cover the pot and simmer for 15 to 20 minutes.

5. Add the raisins and cashews and stir well. Remove from the heat and let cool for about 10 minutes. Fluff with a fork and serve.

You can accompany this with traditional spicy Goan chorizo on the side and with roast pork and a mango salad.

INGREDIENTS

SERVES 6

2 cups **basmati rice**

¼ cup **olive oil**

1 cup diced **onion**

½ of a **plum tomato**, diced

3 ¾ cups **water**

4 **chicken bouillon cubes**, preferably Knorr brand

¼ teaspoon ground **turmeric**

¼ teaspoon ground **cinnamon**

¼ teaspoon ground **black pepper**

¼ teaspoon ground **cloves**

1 cup frozen **peas**

½ cup **raisins**

½ cup shelled **cashews**

JULY 25

ST. CHRISTOPHER

— Turkey —

Born: circa 220, Died: circa 250

The name Christopher means "Christ-bearer," a title that reflects the most famous story about him. According to tradition, he once carried a small child across a rising river. As they reached the other side, the child revealed Himself as Christ, explaining that Christopher had also carried the weight of the world on his shoulders.

A towering figure both physically and spiritually, St. Christopher traveled far to evangelize and spread the Faith. In Lycia (modern-day Turkey), he witnessed, and experienced, Christians being persecuted for the Faith. St. Christopher was eventually arrested and ordered to participate in pagan worship. Refusing to renounce his faith, he converted two women sent to tempt him. Enraged, the emperor ordered his execution—either by beheading or arrows. His martyrdom is believed to have occurred around A.D. 251.

Though details of his life remain uncertain, his legacy as a defender of the Faith and protector of travelers remains strong. His feast day, celebrated on July 25, reminds us to trust in Christ's strength to guide us through life's turbulent waters.

SPANAKOPITA

THE RECIPE DONOR EXPLAINED THE CHOICE of a Greek entrée for St. Christopher: "There is an epic of St. Christopher that says he was martyred in Lycia. Lycia changed hands a few times between the Persians and the Greeks. Since Christopher's name is Greek in origin, we suspect he may have been Greek. Of course, we aren't 100% sure, but that's why we went with a Greek dish."

INGREDIENTS

SERVES 6 TO 8

2 tablespoons **olive oil**, divided

32-ounce package fresh **spinach**, rinsed and washed

½ cup finely chopped **onion**

½ cup thinly sliced **green onions**

2 tablespoons finely chopped fresh **parsley**

2 tablespoons finely chopped **fresh dill**

1 teaspoon minced **garlic**

8 ounces **feta cheese**, crumbled

1 **egg**, lightly beaten

Salt and freshly ground **black pepper**, to taste

1 package **frozen phyllo dough sheets**, thawed

¾ cup **butter**, melted

1. Preheat the oven to 375 degrees F. Line a sheet pan with parchment paper and set aside.

2. Heat 1 tablespoon of olive oil in a large pan over medium heat. Add half the spinach to the pan and cook until wilted. Add the remaining spinach to the pan. Cook for 3 to 4 minutes more until all of the spinach is wilted. Remove the spinach from the pan and let it cool. Wring out excess water and coarsely chop the spinach.

3. Wipe out the pan with a paper towel. Heat the remaining tablespoon of olive oil over medium heat. Add the onion and cook for 3 to 4 minutes or until softened. Stir in the green onions, garlic, parsley, and dill and cook for 30 seconds.

4. Transfer the onion mixture to a bowl along with the chopped spinach, feta cheese, and egg. Season with salt and pepper, to taste. Stir it until thoroughly combined.

5. Take the phyllo dough out of the package and unroll it onto a flat surface. Keep the phyllo covered with a damp towel when not working with it. Lay out one sheet of dough with the long end facing you. Brush the melted butter over the dough. Add a second layer of dough on top of the first, then brush the second layer with butter.

6. Cut the dough vertically into 3-inch-wide strips. Place 1 ½ teaspoons of filling on one end of the dough strip. Fold one corner of the dough over the filling to make a triangle shape. Fold the strip of dough over itself, like how you would fold a flag, until you reach the end. Brush a little melted butter over the top and place the triangle on the prepared sheet pan. Repeat the process with the remaining dough and filling. Arrange the triangles 1 ½ inches apart on the sheet pans.

7. Bake for 18 to 20 minutes or until golden brown. Serve warm.

JULY 25

ST. JAMES
THE APOSTLE

— Israel —

Born: Early first century, Died: circa 44

St. James the Greater, one of Jesus' twelve apostles, was the brother of John and the son of Zebedee. He was among the first disciples to follow Christ and was present at key moments in His ministry, including the Transfiguration. As a passionate and bold preacher of the gospel, James traveled to Spain, spreading Christianity before returning to Jerusalem, where he became the first apostle to be martyred around A.D. 44.

His remains are believed to rest in Santiago de Compostela, now a major pilgrimage site for the famous Camino de Santiago. St. James is often depicted with a walking staff and scallop shell, symbols of pilgrimage and faith.

His feast day, celebrated on July 25, is a joyous occasion in Spain and beyond, often marked with seafood dishes and Galician specialties, like *tarta de Santiago* (almond cake). As you prepare your feast, remember St. James's unwavering devotion and his call to follow Christ with courage and perseverance.

TARTA DE SANTIAGO (SPANISH ALMOND CAKE OR ST. JAMES CAKE)

THIS CAKE, WHICH DATES BACK TO the Middle Ages, is a symbol of Galician heritage and features the iconic Cross of St. James dusted atop, celebrating the region's deep-rooted connection to the Camino de Santiago pilgrimage.

1. Preheat the oven to 350 degrees F. Grease a 10-inch springform pan with butter and set aside.

2. Pulse the almonds in a food processor until finely ground—do not overprocess and turn the mixture into almond butter. Beat the sugar and eggs until the mixture is pale and creamy, then add the lemon zest, liquor, and cinnamon. Fold in the ground almonds using a rubber spatula and pour the almond cake batter into the springform pan.

3. Bake for 30 to 40 minutes, or until the cake is golden brown and a toothpick comes out clean. If the cake is not done at 30 minutes, cover the cake with aluminum foil and bake for 5 more minutes, then test again.

4. Remove from the oven and allow the cake to cool in the pan. Then transfer to a serving dish. Place the cutout of the cross of St. James on top of the cake. Decorate with a sprinkling of confectioners' sugar and remove the cutout cross. Serve the cake in slices with the fresh fruit, if desired.

Be sure to photocopy a Cross of St. James found in Appendix III and cut it out before you start!

INGREDIENTS

SERVES 8 TO 10

Butter, for greasing the pan

2 cups **shelled and blanched almonds**, toasted if desired

1 ¼ cups **granulated sugar**

5 large **eggs**

Lemon zest from half a lemon

1 tablespoon **orujo** (Galician grape liquor), **vodka**, **Cointreau**, **amaretto**, **grappa**, or **vanilla** or **almond extract**

1 teaspoon ground **cinnamon**

TOPPINGS

Confectioners' sugar, for dusting

Fresh fruit, optional

AUGUST 14

ST. MAXIMILIAN KOLBE

— Poland —

Born: 1894, Died: 1941

Born in 1894 in what is now Poland, St. Maximilian Kolbe was deeply devoted to the Virgin Mary from a young age. At the age of twelve, he had a vision of Our Lady offering him two crowns — one white for purity and one red for martyrdom. He accepted both.

Joining the Conventual Franciscans at the age of thirteen, he was ordained a priest in 1918 and tirelessly promoted Marian devotion, founding the Militia of the Immaculata and publishing Rycerz Niepokalanej (Knight of the *Immaculata*). His missionary zeal led him to establish monasteries in Poland, Japan, and India.

During World War II, he sheltered Jewish refugees before being arrested and sent to Auschwitz. There, he offered his life in place of a condemned prisoner, enduring two weeks of starvation before receiving a lethal injection. He died on August 14, 1941, his last words were "Ave Maria."

And his feast day, on August 14, calls us to reflect on selfless love. Honoring his legacy, a feast might include simple Polish dishes — like pierogi.

PIEROGI

As one of the many great Polish saints, St. Maximilian Kolbe is fittingly celebrated with a pierogi feast. Since these beloved Polish dumplings date back to the seventeenth century in Poland, we can be fairly certain that the saint partook of them himself.

1. To make the filling, place the potatoes in a pot, cover them with water, and cook until tender. Once they are tender, use a potato ricer or potato masher to mash the potatoes so they have no lumps. Add the cream cheese, cheddar cheese, green onions, salt, and pepper. Mix to combine.

2. To make the dough, in a large bowl add the flour and salt. Make a little well in the middle and start adding milk and butter. Stir gently to incorporate. Add a little water at a time and work the dough until you can form a ball, about 5 minutes. Cover with plastic wrap and let it rest for 20 minutes.

3. On a lightly floured surface, turn out the dough and roll until the thickness of pasta, about ⅛-inch thick. Use a round cookie cutter or a large drinking glass to cut out 2–inch circles. Place one teaspoon of the potato filling in the center of each circle. Wet the outer edges of the circle with water, fold in half, and then seal the edges by pinching them together or by using a fork to crimp around the edge of the pierogi.

4. Bring water to a boil in a large pot and season with salt. Put about 8 pierogi in at a time. Once they come to the surface, let them cook for 1 minute. Then use a slotted spoon to transfer to a paper towel-lined plate. In a large skillet, add 2 tablespoons of butter and heat over medium-high. Pan-fry the boiled pierogi in batches until lightly browned on both sides, about 2 minutes per side.

INGREDIENTS

SERVES 6 TO 8

FILLING

2 large **Russet potatoes**, peeled and diced

1/2 tablespoon **butter**

4 ounces **cream cheese**

¼ cup shredded **cheddar cheese**

3 **green onion stalks**, sliced

Kosher salt and freshly ground **black pepper**, to taste

DOUGH

3 cups **all-purpose flour**

A pinch of **salt**

½ cup **whole milk**, warmed

1 tablespoon **unsalted butter**, melted; plus 2 tablespoons butter for frying

½ to ¾ cup **warm water** (depending on how much your flour soaks)

Let Us Pray

Remember, O most gracious Virgin Mary, that never was it known that anyone who fled to your protection, implored your help, or sought your intercession, was left unaided. Inspired by this confidence, I fly unto you, O Virgin of virgins, my Mother. To you do I come, before you I stand, sinful and sorrowful. O Mother of the Word Incarnate, despise not my petitions, but in your mercy, hear and answer me. Amen.

SOLEMNITY OF THE ASSUMPTION OF THE BLESSED VIRGIN MARY

— Holy Day of Obligation —

AUGUST 15

The feast of the Assumption, celebrated on August 15, honors the dogma that Our Lady was taken up, body and soul, into heavenly glory.

In *Munificentissimus Deus* (1950), Pope Pius XII proclaimed this teaching as a divinely revealed dogma, declaring: "The Immaculate Mother of God, the ever Virgin Mary, having completed the course of her earthly life, was assumed body and soul into heavenly glory." This solemn declaration strengthened the faithful's hope in their own resurrection, uniting belief in Mary's Assumption with the promise of eternal life.

Rooted in the 1854 dogma of the Immaculate Conception, which proclaimed Mary free from Original Sin, the Assumption has been venerated since the early centuries of Christianity. Writings as early as the fifth century suggest devotion to this mystery, with texts like *Liber Requiei Mariae (Book of Mary's Repose)* providing some of the earliest narratives about Mary's passing and Assumption.

Whether she experienced bodily death or was taken directly to Heaven remains a mystery, but the Assumption of Mary is a powerful testament to God's victory over sin and death—a foreshadowing of the resurrection promised to all who follow Christ.

ASSUMPTA SALAD

This bright, refreshing salad is the perfect appetizer for your family feast on this solemnity. Perhaps enjoy a beautiful summer picnic after attending Mass.

1. Whisk the vinaigrette ingredients together until thickened. Let stand for about 1 hour.

2. For the salad, arrange tomato slices on 6 to 8 salad plates. Sprinkle the onion and olives among them. Sprinkle the herbs evenly, then add the cheese cubes in the middle of each dish. Whisk the vinaigrette just before serving and drizzle evenly over each plate. Serve immediatcly.

INGREDIENTS

SERVES 6 TO 8

VINAIGRETTE

½ cup plus 2 tablespoons **extra-virgin olive oil**

5 tablespoons **red wine vinegar**

1 **garlic** clove, peeled and minced

Salt and freshly ground **black pepper**, to taste

SALAD

8 medium-sized ripe **tomatoes**, sliced

1 **red onion**, finely chopped

1 cup **pitted black** or **kalamata olives**, drained

⅓ cup chopped fresh **basil**

¼ cup chopped fresh **oregano**

¼ cup fresh **Italian parsley**

1 cup cubed **feta cheese**

AUGUST 23

ST. ROSE OF LIMA

— Peru —

Born: 1586, Died: 1617

Born in Lima, Peru, in 1586, St. Rose of Lima was originally named Isabel Flores de Olivia. Her striking beauty earned her the nickname "Rose," inspired by a legend in which a servant saw her face transform into a radiant rose. She officially adopted the name in 1597, at her confirmation.

From a young age, Rose was deeply devoted to God, practicing prayer, fasting, and penance in secret. She rejected suitors by cutting her hair and damaging her complexion, choosing instead a life of chastity and sacrifice. At the age of twenty, she joined the Third Order of St. Dominic, living in a secluded hut where she wore a crown of thorns and dedicated herself to caring for the sick and poor.

Rose supported the needy by selling her embroidery and flowers from her family's garden. She passed away at just thirty-one on August 24, 1617. Canonized in 1671, she became the first saint of the Americas. Today, she is the patroness of embroiderers, florists, gardeners, and Latin America.

CEVICHE

Ceviche, the national dish of Peru, was apparently created nearly two thousand years ago, and the ancient natives at the time "cooked" the raw fish with the juice of local fruit, possibly passion fruit. When preparing this delicious dish, cooks can choose from fresh cod, swordfish, rockfish, or small shrimp. Feel free to adjust the quantities based on the amount of fish being used. You will need enough limes for the juice to cover the fish completely in the bowl while it is marinating.

1. Slice the fish across the grain ¼-inch thick. Then cut each piece into 1-inch squares. Place the pieces in a nonreactive bowl, and sprinkle with the coarse salt. Allow to rest for about 30 minutes.

2. Pour the lime juice over the fish and toss until all the pieces are equally soaked in the juice. The lime juice should completely cover the fish.

3. Meanwhile, slice the jalapeños in half lengthwise, and remove the stems and the seeds. Dice the jalapeños and add to the bowl with the fish. Add the crushed garlic, chopped cilantro, and diced tomatoes, and stir into the mixture. Add the diced avocados, if using, and stir the mixture again.

4. Refrigerate the mixture for at least one hour, as the fish "cooks" in the lime juice. Toss every 15 to 30 minutes to ensure equal contact between the lime juice and the fish. After one hour, remove from the refrigerator and serve. Enjoy!

INGREDIENTS

SERVES 4 TO 6

2 to 3 pounds fresh **cod**

3 to 4 tablespoons **coarse salt**

20 **limes**, juiced

5 **jalapeño peppers**

2 cloves fresh **garlic**, peeled and crushed

1 bunch fresh **cilantro**, chopped

2 to 4 fresh **tomatoes**, diced

2 **avocados**, peeled and diced, optional

AUGUST 24

ST. BARTHOLOMEW

— Israel —

Born: Early first century, Died: circa 70

St. Bartholomew, also known as Nathaniel, was one of the twelve apostles. Introduced to Jesus by St. Philip, he initially doubted, asking, "Can anything good come out of Nazareth?" (John 1:46). Yet, upon meeting him, Christ declared, "Behold, an Israelite indeed, in whom is no guile!" (John 1:47). This encounter transformed Bartholomew into a devoted follower of Christ.

After the Ascension, he traveled as a missionary, preaching in Mesopotamia, Parthia, Ethiopia, India, and Armenia. Tradition holds that he was martyred in Armenia, either by beheading or being flayed alive before crucifixion. His relics eventually found their way to Rome, where they remain enshrined today.

St. Bartholomew is the patron saint of plasterers. His steadfast faith reminds us to trust in Christ, even when doubts arise.

BARTLEMAS BEEF

TRADITIONALLY, THE BEEF SERVED ON THIS day was known as Bartlemas Beef (*Bartlemas* means the "Mass of St. Bartholomew"). The following recipe is given in *Cook's Guide* from 1664. If you can, prepare the brisket a day before cooking it; that gives it time to soak up the flavors from the dry rub. Plan to serve this hot with parsnips and potatoes.

1. Refrigerate the brisket one day before preparation. To prepare, remove the brisket from the refrigerator. Use paper towels to pat the brisket dry. Take the dry rub spices and massage them vigorously into the meat on all sides. Wrap the brisket in foil and return it to the refrigerator overnight.

2. Eight hours before serving (it'll cook for 7) the brisket, remove it from the refrigerator and let it get to room temperature. In a Dutch oven on the stove, brown the brisket on medium-high heat on all sides, then set aside. In the same Dutch oven, sauté the chopped onions in olive oil on medium heat for about 10 minutes. Add the minced garlic and continue sautéing for 1 to 2 minutes. Add half of the wine and half of the broth and stir well, gently scraping the bottom of the pan.

3. Preheat the oven to 300 degrees F. Return the brisket to the Dutch oven, fat side on top. Add a tight-fitting lid and place into the preheated oven. The liquid should reach halfway up the brisket. Add more, if needed.

4. Braise for 1 hour and 15 minutes per pound—the meat will be done at this point but will increase in tenderness if braised for an additional 2 to 3 hours. Every 30 minutes or so, ladle some of the cooking liquid over the top of the brisket. Have the broth and wine standing by, in case you need to add more. The bottom half of the brisket should be surrounded by liquid. Add water if you run out of wine and broth.

5. To make the gravy, remove the roast and set aside. Bring the braising liquid to a boil over medium heat. Make a cornstarch slurry by combining 1 tablespoon of cornstarch with 2 tablespoons of water. Add the slurry to the braising liquid until it reaches your desired consistency. Spoon the glaze over the brisket slices before serving.

INGREDIENTS

SERVES 6

About 3 ½ pounds **brisket of beef**

Olive oil

1 large **sweet onion**, peeled and chopped, or 6 **shallots**, chopped

6 to 8 cloves of **garlic**, peeled and minced

1 bottle **Chianti** or **Merlot wine**

1 box (32 fluid ounces) **beef, chicken, or vegetable broth**

Possibly some **water**

Possibly some **cornstarch** to thicken broth

DRY RUB

Thoroughly mix together the following spices:

1 teaspoon **salt**

½ teaspoon ground **nutmeg**

½ teaspoon ground **ginger**

½ teaspoon ground **cinnamon**

½ teaspoon ground **cloves**

½ teaspoon ground **mace** (see note)

If you cannot find mace, increase the amount of nutmeg to 1 teaspoon.

SEPTEMBER 5

ST. TERESA
OF CALCUTTA

— India —

Born: 1910, Died: 1997

Born in 1910 in Skopje, Macedonia, St. Teresa of Calcutta — widely known as Mother Teresa — was raised in a devout Catholic family. Drawn to missionary work, she joined the Sisters of Loreto in Ireland in 1928 and soon moved to Calcutta, India, where she became a teacher and later the principal of St. Mary's School.

In 1946, during a train ride to Darjeeling, she experienced a divine calling to serve "the poorest of the poor." This led her to establish the Missionaries of Charity in 1950, dedicated to caring for the sick, abandoned, and dying. Her work expanded worldwide, including in communist countries, and she founded additional ministries, such as the Corpus Christi Movement for Priests.

Mother Teresa's selfless service earned global recognition, including the Nobel Peace Prize in 1979. Despite declining health, she remained devoted to her mission until her passing in 1997. Canonized in 2016, she is the patron saint of World Youth Day and the Missionaries of Charity. Her legacy continues to inspire countless acts of love and service.

NAAN FLATBREAD

Soft, pillowy, and rich in tradition, naan bread has been a staple of Indian cuisine for centuries. Its origins trace back to ancient Persia before becoming popular in India, where it's baked in clay ovens for a signature charred flavor. A fitting recipe for a feast celebrating service, it reminds us that simple, shared meals can be acts of love.

1. Pour the milk into a large liquid measuring glass and heat in the microwave until warm to the touch (approximately 110 degrees F).

2. Add the heated milk into a mixing bowl and sprinkle with the yeast and sugar. Allow this mixture to rest for 4 to 5 minutes until the yeast begins to bubble. Add 2 ½ cups of flour and 1 teaspoon of salt. Mix well to combine.

3. Gradually add the flour in small amounts, until a soft dough is formed, about 3 to 5 minutes. You'll know you're done when the dough starts cleaning the sides of the bowl. It should be smooth and elastic. Place the dough in a lightly greased bowl and let it rest at room temperature, covered lightly with a towel, for 2 hours.

4. After the dough has rested, turn it onto a lightly floured surface and divide the dough into 16 equal portions, rounding each into a ball shape. One by one, roll out each dough ball into a 4- to 5-inch circle.

5. On a cooktop over medium-high heat, heat a large ungreased skillet or griddle pan. Place the flattened dough rounds directly onto the hot surface and allow the underside to brown, about 2 to 3 minutes—the top should puff and bubble. Once the bottom has browned, flip the naan over to brown on the other side. Remove from the skillet and brush lightly with the softened butter. If desired, add a sprinkle of garlic powder to the softened butter. Continue with the remaining dough.

INGREDIENTS

SERVES 16

1 ½ cups **whole milk**

½ teaspoon **active dry yeast**

1 teaspoon **granulated sugar**

3 to 4 cups **all-purpose flour**

1 teaspoon **salt**

3 tablespoons **butter**, softened, for finishing

Sprinkle of **garlic powder** (optional)

You can easily double the recipe and freeze the dough for later use.

EXALTATION OF THE HOLY CROSS

— Israel —

The Feast of the Exaltation of the Holy Cross dates back to the fourth century when St. Helena, mother of Emperor Constantine, traveled to Jerusalem in search of Christ's sacred sites. During her journey, she ordered the demolition of a pagan temple built over Christ's tomb. Beneath it, three crosses were discovered, and one—believed to be Christ's—was identified when a sick person was miraculously healed upon touching it.

To honor this discovery, Constantine built the Church of the Holy Sepulchre over the site. By the late fourth century, Christians in Jerusalem venerated the Cross on Good Friday, bowing, touching, and kissing it in devotion. In the seventh century, after the Persians had taken the Cross as a war prize, Emperor Heraclius recovered and restored it, solidifying its role as a powerful symbol of faith.

Today, the cross remains central to Christian devotion, represented in art, jewelry, and liturgical processions. The Sign of the Cross is a profession of faith, reminding the faithful of Christ's sacrifice.

HOT CROSS BUNS

THE ORIGIN AND HISTORY OF HOT cross buns are unclear. Some records claim that Christian monks made them to give to the poor. Apparently, one monk etched a cross on the bun, and that today is still a popular representation of these sweet treats. The cross represents the Crucifixion of Christ, and the spices baked into each bun signify the spices used to embalm Our Lord.

1. Lightly grease a 10-inch square pan or 9-inch x 13-inch pan and set aside. Mix the apple juice or rum with the dried fruit and raisins or currants and heat over medium heat just until the fruit is very warm. Allow to cool to room temperature.

2. Weigh your flour; or measure it by gently spooning it into a measuring cup, then leveling off any excess. Mix together the flour and all of the remaining dough ingredients (including the eggs and the egg yolk from the separated egg). Knead the mixture, using an electric mixer or bread machine, until the dough is soft and elastic. It'll be very loose, sticking to the bottom of the bowl and your hands as you work with it—lightly greasing your hands will make your job easier. Mix in the cooled fruit and any liquid not absorbed by the fruit.

3. Let the dough rise for 1 hour, covered. It should become puffy, though may not double in size.

4. Divide the dough into 12 to 14 pieces that weigh 3 ¾ ounces each, about the size of a billiard ball. Use your greased hands to round them into balls. Arrange them in the prepared pan. Cover the pan, and let the buns rise for 1 hour, or until they've puffed up and are touching one another. While the dough is rising, preheat the oven to 375 degrees F. Whisk together the reserved egg white and milk and brush it over the buns.

5. Bake the buns for 30 minutes, until they're golden brown. Remove from the oven, carefully turn the buns out of the pan (they should come out in one large piece), and transfer them to a rack to cool. Mix together the icing ingredients. When the buns are completely cool, pipe a cross shape atop each bun.

INGREDIENTS

MAKES 12 TO 14 BUNS

BUNS

¼ cup **apple juice** or **rum**

½ cup **dried fruit** of your choice

½ cup **raisins** or **dried currants**

4 ½ cups **all-purpose flour**

1 ¼ cups **milk**, at room temperature

2 large **eggs**, plus 1 **egg yolk** (save the white for the topping)

6 tablespoons **butter**, at room temperature

2 teaspoons **instant yeast**

¼ cup **light brown sugar**, packed

1 tablespoon **baking powder**

1 ¾ teaspoons **table salt**

1 teaspoon ground **cinnamon**

¼ teaspoon ground **cloves** or **allspice**

¼ teaspoon ground **nutmeg**

TOPPING

1 large **egg white**, reserved from above

1 tablespoon **milk**

ICING

1 cup plus 2 tablespoons **confectioners' sugar**

½ teaspoon **vanilla extract**

Pinch of **table salt**

4 teaspoons **milk**, or enough to make a thick, pipable icing

SEPTEMBER 21

ST. MATTHEW
THE APOSTLE

— *Israel* —

Born: First century,
Died: Late first century

St. Matthew, the son of Alphaeus, was a tax collector in Capernaum when Jesus called him, saying, "Follow me" (Matt. 9:9). Leaving everything behind, he became one of the twelve apostles and later the author of the first Gospel. St. Matthew's Gospel was originally composed in Aramaic for Jewish Christians, affirming Jesus as the long-awaited Messiah. Jesus was unlike the militant leader many expected, and His Kingdom was spiritual, fulfilling the prophecies in a new and profound way. Early theologians, including Origen, recognized Matthew as the first to record the good news.

Little is known about St. Matthew's later life. Tradition suggests he preached in Parthia, Persia, or Ethiopia, but his death remains a mystery—whether natural or by martyrdom. He is often depicted with a human figure, one of the four living creatures from Revelation, symbolizing Christ's humanity.

St. Matthew is the patron saint of bankers, accountants, and bookkeepers. His life is a testament to the power of conversion and the spreading of God's Word.

ST. MATTHEW SILVER DOLLAR PANCAKES

THESE SILVER DOLLAR PANCAKES REMIND US of St. Matthew's early life as a tax collector—when he would have undoubtedly handled his fair share of silver coins. As the recipe donor noted, you can use icing to decorate coin designs onto your pancakes.

1. Mix the flour, sugar, baking powder, baking soda, and salt in a large bowl.

2. Whisk the buttermilk and eggs together, then pour into the dry ingredients. Gently combine with a rubber spatula. Do not over-mix. Some lumps are fine. The batter can be refrigerated for an hour or two, if desired.

3. Heat a griddle or skillet over low heat for about 5 minutes. Lightly spray it with cooking spray. Working in batches, drop tablespoon-fuls onto the skillet. Cook over low heat until bubbles appear on the top and a few have burst, about 2 minutes. Flip and cook on underside until browned, about 1 minute. Repeat with the remaining batter, spraying the skillet between every few batches. Serve hot with desired toppings.

INGREDIENTS

SERVES 4 TO 6

2 cups **all-purpose flour**

2 tablespoons **granulated sugar**

1 ½ teaspoons **baking powder**

1 ½ teaspoons **baking soda**

½ teaspoon **salt**

2 ½ cups **buttermilk**

2 large **eggs**

Nonstick cooking spray

STS. MICHAEL, GABRIEL, AND RAPHAEL, ARCHANGELS

September 29

Celebrated on September 29, the feast of the Archangels honors Sts. Michael, Gabriel, and Raphael, the only three angels named in Scripture. Originally dedicated solely to St. Michael, the feast was expanded after Vatican II to include all three, highlighting their unique missions and shared role in God's divine plan.

The term archangel comes from the Greek *arkhángelos*, meaning "chief angel," signifying their leadership over other heavenly beings. Each archangel has a distinct role in salvation history.

St. Michael, the great warrior and defender of the Church, is often depicted with a sword, standing over Satan. His name means "Who is like God?" and he is invoked for protection against evil.

St. Gabriel, God's messenger, announced the Incarnation to the Virgin Mary. His name means "Strength of God," and he is the patron of messengers, broadcasters, and postal workers.

St. Raphael, the healer, guided Tobias in the book of Tobit. His name means "God heals," and he is the patron of travelers, the sick, and healthcare workers.

As we honor these heavenly protectors, we are reminded of their continued presence and intercession in our daily lives.

MICHAELMAS PIE

HISTORICALLY, THIS HEARTY DISH MARKED THE culmination of harvest season and symbolized the protection and guidance provided by the archangels. If you're feeling creative, try cutting out an angel or archangel shape for your top pie crust.

1. Prepare the pastry by placing the flour in a large bowl and stir in the cinnamon and salt. Rub in the lard and butter with your fingertips until the mixture resembles fine breadcrumbs. Make a well in the center and add the chilled water. Bring the mixture together using a butter knife. Once it has come together, knead for a brief moment and place it in a plastic bag in the refrigerator. Leave to rest for 30 minutes.

2. Peel and core the apples. Cut them into large chunks and place them in a saucepan with the sugar, nutmeg, and cloves. Cover with a lid and gently cook for 5 minutes, until the apples have softened. Fold in the blackberries and remove the saucepan from the heat. Cool completely.

3. Preheat the oven to 350 degrees F. Remove the pastry bag from the refrigerator and roll out two-thirds on a lightly floured surface. Add the bottom crust to an 8-inch glass or ceramic pie plate or an 8-inch parchment-lined metal pie plate. Prick the base of the pastry with a fork. Strain the fruit, reserving the juices, and spoon the fruit mixture into the prepared pie plate.

4. Roll out the remaining pastry. Lay the pastry over the fruit. Lift back the edge and brush the base with a little beaten egg and seal the edge. Trim and crimp the pastry edges. Brush the surface with the remaining egg and make a couple of slits in the top. Sprinkle a little sugar over the pastry.

5. Bake for 35 minutes. Serve hot or cold, with ice cream or fresh whipped cream.

INGREDIENTS

SERVES 4 TO 6

2 ½ cups **all-purpose flour,** sifted

½ teaspoon ground **cinnamon**

Pinch **salt**

8 tablespoons **lard**

8 tablespoons **chilled butter,** diced

½ cup **chilled water**

2 pounds **cooking apples**

¼ cup **granulated sugar,** plus extra for sprinkling on the top

1 teaspoon ground **nutmeg**

½ teaspoon ground **cloves**

¾ pound **blackberries**

1 **egg,** beaten

THE HOLY GUARDIAN ANGELS

October 2

Celebrated on October 2, the Feast of the Guardian Angels is a beautiful reminder of God's loving care for each of us. From the moment of our birth, God assigns us a guardian angel—a heavenly protector who guides, watches over, and intercedes for us throughout our lives.

The belief in guardian angels is deeply rooted in Scripture. In Matthew 18:10, Jesus says, "See that you do not despise one of these little ones; for I tell you that in heaven their angels always behold the face of my Father who is in heaven." This passage affirms that these celestial companions are ever present, offering divine guidance and protection.

Devotion to guardian angels has been cherished throughout Church history. In the seventeenth century, Pope Paul V established it as a universal feast, encouraging the faithful to recognize and honor these unseen but ever-faithful friends. The tradition of praying the guardian angel prayer is a simple yet powerful way to acknowledge their presence.

As we celebrate this feast, we are reminded to trust in God's providence and to listen to the gentle promptings of our guardian angels, who lead us ever closer to Him.

ANGEL DELIGHT

The "heavenly" dessert—made from a combination of angel food cake and a
creamy, luscious filling—is a fitting reminder of our heavenly friends.

1. Mix the gelatin with ½ cup milk and heat over medium heat,
   stirring to dissolve.

2. Blend the cream cheese with the remaining milk until smooth.
   Add the sugar, almond extract, and the milk with gelatin and fold
   into the Cool Whip.

3. Tear the cake into bite-sized pieces and place them in a flat cake
   pan. Pour the milk mixture over the top and spread the pie filling
   over the top. Refrigerate until set.

INGREDIENTS

SERVES 10 TO 12

1 envelope **unflavored gelatin**

1 ½ cups **milk**

8 ounces **cream cheese**

½ cup **granulated sugar**

1 teaspoon **almond extract**

8-ounce container of **Cool Whip**

1 **precooked angel food cake**

2 cans **pie filling** of your choice

OCTOBER 4

ST. FRANCIS OF ASSISI

— Italy —

Born: 1181, Died: 1226

Born in 1181 in Assisi, Italy, St. Francis was originally named Giovanni but was later called Francesco by his father, a wealthy cloth merchant. As a young man, he lived a life of luxury and revelry, but he longed for something greater. He sought glory as a knight, but after a battle and imprisonment, he returned home disillusioned.

A turning point came when Francis heard God's call at the Church of San Damiano, urging him to "rebuild my church." At first, he took this literally, using his father's money to restore the crumbling building. However, through prayer, he realized his true mission was to renew the Church spiritually. He renounced his wealth, embraced poverty, and dedicated his life to preaching, serving the poor, and caring for God's creation.

Francis established the Franciscan Order in 1209. In 1224, he received the stigmata, miraculously bearing Christ's wounds. He died in 1226 at age forty-four, leaving a legacy of devotion and holy simplicity.

St. Francis is the patron saint of animals, ecology, and Italy, reminding us of the beauty of God's world and the call to live with joy and compassion.

POOR MAN'S CAKE

POOR MAN'S CAKE IS A HUMBLE yet delicious treat that captures the spirit of St. Francis, reflecting his life of simplicity and love for the poor. This recipe, packed with nourishing ingredients like raisins and walnuts, offers a sweet way to remember his teachings as you celebrate.

1. Preheat the oven to 325 degrees F. Grease and flour a Bundt or ring pan and set aside.

2. Place the water, brown sugar, raisins, shortening, cinnamon, and cloves in a saucepan over medium heat. Bring to a boil and boil for 5 minutes. Remove from the heat and cool completely.

3. Mix the flour and baking powder in a large bowl. Dissolve the baking soda in 1 teaspoon of water. Add the raisin mixture and baking soda mixture to the flour mixture. Fold in the nuts. Spoon into the prepared pan.

4. Bake for 50 minutes to one hour, until a toothpick inserted into the middle comes out clean (ring pans might require less time than Bundt pans). Remove from the oven and cool for 15 minutes. Turn the cake out of the pan and cool completely on a baking rack.

5. In a bowl, mix the melted butter with confectioners' sugar, milk, and vanilla extract until smooth and a thick drizzling consistency. Add a little more milk if necessary. Spoon over the crown of the cake, allowing it to drip down the sides.

INGREDIENTS

SERVES 8 TO 10

CAKE
2 cups **water**

1 cup **brown sugar**, packed

2 cups **raisins**

⅓ cup **shortening**

1 teaspoon ground **cinnamon**

1 teaspoon ground **cloves**

3 cups **all-purpose flour**

½ teaspoon **baking powder**

1 teaspoon **baking soda**

1 cup shelled **walnuts**

GLAZE
2 tablespoons **butter**, melted

2 cups **confectioners' sugar**

2 to 4 tablespoons **milk**

1 teaspoon **vanilla extract**

OCTOBER 22

POPE ST. JOHN PAUL II

— Poland —

Born: 1920, Died: 2005

Born in Wadowice, Poland, in 1920, Karol Józef Wojtyła's journey to sainthood was marked by resilience and deep faith. After the Nazi occupation forced his university to close, he secretly studied for the priesthood while working in a quarry. Ordained in 1946, he earned a doctorate in theology in Rome before returning to Poland as a parish priest, professor, and, later, auxiliary bishop of Kraków.

In 1978, Cardinal Wojtyła became Pope John Paul II, launching one of the most influential pontificates in history. With a fearless missionary spirit, he traveled the globe spreading the gospel, advocating for peace, and playing a key role in the fall of Communism in Eastern Europe. He survived an assassination attempt in 1981 and later forgave his attacker.

A champion of mercy, he instituted the Great Jubilee of 2000 and established Divine Mercy Sunday—on which he passed away in 2005. Canonized in 2014, Pope St. John Paul II remains a beloved patron of youth, families, and Poland. His legacy endures in the Church's call to holiness and unity.

KREMÓWKA PAPIESKA (POLISH CREAM CAKE)

POLISH CREAM CAKE, AFFECTIONATELY KNOWN AS "Pope's Cake," gained fame when Pope John Paul II shared that it was one of his favorite desserts from his homeland. As the story goes, the Polish pontiff was gifted copious amounts of this sweet treat during a visit to Poland in 1999.

INGREDIENTS

SERVES 8 TO 10

CREAM FILLING

1 ½ cups **granulated sugar**

¼ cup **cornstarch**

¼ teaspoon **salt**

4 whole **egg yolks**

3 cups **whole milk**

2 tablespoons **butter**

2 teaspoons **vanilla extract**

WHIPPED CREAM

1 cup **heavy cream**, well chilled

2 tablespoons **confectioners' sugar**, plus ¼ cup for dusting

1 teaspoon **vanilla extract**

1. Preheat the oven to 425 degrees F. To prepare the puff pastry, line two sheet pans with parchment paper. Place the puff pastries on the parchment-lined sheet pans. Using a fork, dock both puff pastries. Top the puff pastries with more parchment paper and place an upside-down cooling rake over the sheet pan to prevent the puff pastries from puffing up too much in the oven. Bake for 15 minutes. Remove the parchment and cooling rack and bake for another 2 minutes, or until golden brown. Allow it to cool on a cooling rack until ready to layer.

2. Combine the sugar, cornstarch, and salt in a medium saucepan. Mix to incorporate. Pour in the egg yolks and milk and whisk together.

3. Over medium heat, stir continuously until the mixture barely comes to a boil and becomes thickened (about 6 to 8 minutes). As soon as it starts to bubble and thicken, remove it from the heat. Add the butter and vanilla extract and stir until everything is combined. If necessary, strain to remove any lumps that may have developed. Allow it to cool completely.

4. Combine the heavy cream, confectioners' sugar, and vanilla extract in a medium bowl. Use a hand mixer to whip on high until stiff peaks form.

5. Line an 8-inch x 8-inch pan with parchment paper, with overhang on all sides (this is how you will lift it out of the pan later).

6. Add a layer of puff pastry. If necessary, trim the puff pastry slightly to fit into the pan. Add the cooled cream mixture over the top of the pastry and smooth evenly. Then add the whipped cream and smooth. Top with the other sheet of pastry.

7. Cover it with plastic wrap and chill for about 2 hours to allow it to set. When ready to serve, carefully lift it out of the pan by the parchment paper. Place on a serving plate and dust with confectioners' sugar.

OCTOBER 28

STS. SIMON AND JUDE, APOSTLES

—Israel—

Born: Early first century, Died: 65

St. Simon and St. Jude, both apostles of Jesus Christ, are celebrated together on their shared feast day, October 28th.

St. Simon, often called Simon the Zealot, to distinguish him from Simon Peter, is believed to have preached in Egypt before joining St. Jude in Persia. The appellation "Zealot" was likely a reference to Simon's particular sect of Judaism. St. Jude, also known as Thaddeus, is often addressed as the patron saint of desperate cases and lost causes. Tradition holds that he preached in areas including Syria, Mesopotamia, and Persia, where he made significant conversions and established the early churches in those areas.

According to tradition, both apostles were martyred in Persia. Tradition holds that Simon was sawn in half and Jude was clubbed to death. The feast day of St. Simon and St. Jude is not only a day to remember their martyrdom but also their unyielding commitment to their faith and their tireless work as disciples of Christ.

EGYPTIAN FALAFEL

THIS EGYPTIAN FALAFEL RECIPE IS A nod to St. Simon's apostolic work in Egypt. But falafel is also a traditional Middle Eastern dish and is therefore appropriate for the feast of these two great saints who evangelized in that region.

1. Wash the beans under running water, then place in a deep bowl. Cover with water and let them soak for 2 to 3 hours, changing the water once halfway through. Skip this step if you're using canned beans. Drain the beans and place them in the food processor. Add all remaining ingredients, including the spices, except for the water and egg white.

2. Process until very fine. If you feel the dough texture is rough, add 1 to 2 tablespoons of water at a time and mix until you get a smooth dough.

3. Place the dough in a deep bowl and whisk it hard with an electric mixer or a handheld whisk for about 4 to 5 minutes, until it gets foamy and very airy. The volume should increase by a quarter. With a spoon or rubber spatula, fold in the stiff egg white.

4. Heat the oil in a heavy-bottom skillet or a cast-iron skillet — the oil should be at least ⅓-inch deep. Once the oil has reached 350 degrees F, scoop about 2 tablespoons of the falafel mix, shape into a patty, and drop it into the hot oil. Repeat until the skillet is full, about 3 or 4 times. The falafel should not touch each other. Allow enough space between them to flip them over easily.

5. Fry for 1 ½ to 2 minutes per side until each is browned. Transfer to a paper-lined plate. Serve with tahini dip, tomatoes, pickles, cucumbers, onions, and green salad.

INGREDIENTS

MAKES 14 TO 15 PATTIES

FALAFEL

1 cup **split dry fava beans** or 1 cup canned fava beans

1 **scallion**, both green and white parts, chopped

1 bunch **parsley**, roughly chopped

1 bunch **cilantro**, roughly chopped

2 big **garlic** cloves, peeled

½ teaspoon **baking soda**

½ cup **fava** or **chickpea/ garbanzo flour**, sifted

Several tablespoons of **water**, as needed

1 **egg white**, beaten stiff

About 3 cups **olive oil** for frying, or other oil if preferred

SPICES

1 teaspoon ground **coriander**

1 teaspoon **salt**, or to your taste

½ teaspoon ground **cumin**

6. To make the tahini dip, in a bowl, whisk together the tahini and lemon juice until combined. Slowly whisk in the water until it is smooth and creamy. Add the minced garlic, salt, and cumin. Stir well. Drizzle with extra-virgin olive oil and sprinkle with chopped parsley, if desired. Season to taste.

¼ teaspoon ground **black pepper**

1 to 2 tablespoons **water**

Sesame seeds for dipping, optional

TAHINI DIP

½ cup **tahini**

¼ cup **water** (adjust for desired consistency)

2 tablespoons fresh **lemon juice**

1 clove **garlic**, minced

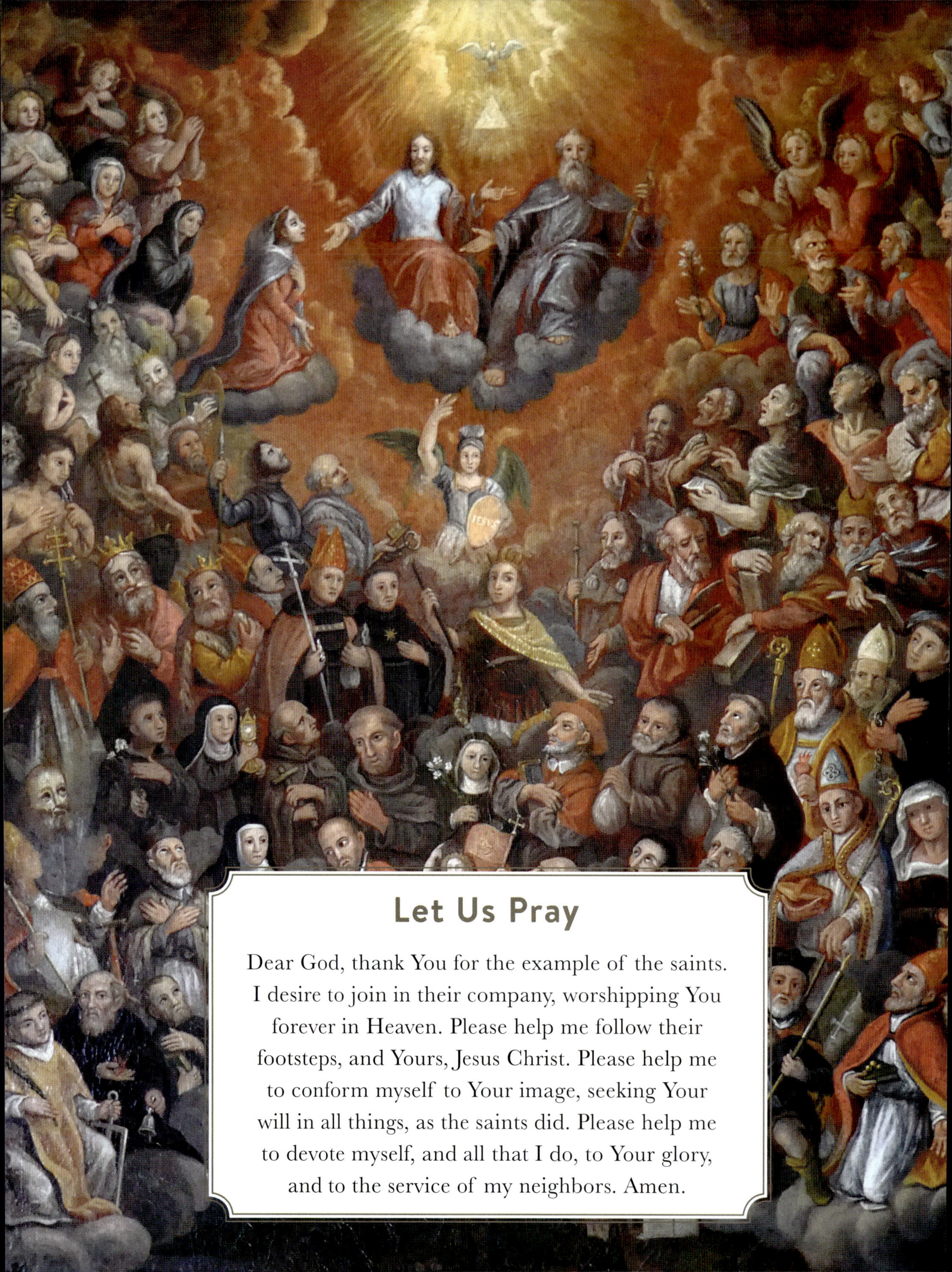

Let Us Pray

Dear God, thank You for the example of the saints. I desire to join in their company, worshipping You forever in Heaven. Please help me follow their footsteps, and Yours, Jesus Christ. Please help me to conform myself to Your image, seeking Your will in all things, as the saints did. Please help me to devote myself, and all that I do, to Your glory, and to the service of my neighbors. Amen.

SOLEMNITY OF ALL SAINTS

NOVEMBER 1

On November 1, the Church triumphantly celebrates All Saints' Day, a solemn feast honoring the countless men and women who now dwell in the glory of Heaven. These saints—both those officially canonized and the many unknown holy souls—have run the race, kept the faith, and now intercede for us before the throne of God. Their lives, filled with sacrifice, virtue, and love for Christ, inspire us to pursue holiness in our own daily walk.

From the earliest centuries, Christians have venerated martyrs and saints, drawing strength from their witness. In the eighth century, Pope Gregory III dedicated a chapel in St. Peter's Basilica to "all the saints," and by the ninth century, All Saints' Day was established as a universal feast. This holy day is a reminder of our call to sainthood, inviting us to reflect on the Communion of Saints—the Church in Heaven, on earth, and in Purgatory—united in Christ's love.

Many cultures have long observed All Saints' Day with special foods and traditions. From soul cakes in England to *panellets* in Spain, families around the world prepare festive meals to honor the saints and share in the joy of their heavenly triumph. As we gather around our tables, let us give thanks for the saints' example and pray for the grace to follow in their footsteps.

All Saints' Day is not only a time of remembrance but also of joy, as we celebrate the victorious lives of those who have gone before us in the Faith. Across generations and cultures, this feast has been marked with prayer, processions, and family gatherings.

ALL SAINTS' DAY COOKIES (OSSA DEI MORTI)

OSSA DEI MORTI, LITERALLY "BONES OF the dead," is a traditional Italian cookie that is served on All Saints' Day. Sometimes, they're even baked in the shape of bones.

1. Preheat the oven to 325 degrees F. Line two baking sheets with parchment paper and set aside.

2. In a medium bowl, whisk together the sugar, egg, and almond extract until blended. Stir in the almonds, flour, baking powder, and salt. Dump the mixture onto the floured surface and gently knead for a minute or two with your hands until smooth. The dough will be sticky.

3. Divide the dough into three pieces and roll each into a 1-inch log. Cut the log into 1 ½-inch to 2-inch pieces. Using your fingers, roll each piece into ropes about 4 inches long. Place the cookies 2 to 3 inches apart on the baking sheets.

4. Bake for 10 to 12 minutes, or until the cookies just begin to brown and the tops feel set. Cool completely, dust with confectioners' sugar, and enjoy.

INGREDIENTS

YIELDS ABOUT A DOZEN COOKIES

1 cup **granulated sugar**

1 **egg**

1 teaspoon **almond extract**

⅔ cup **ground almonds**

½ cup **all-purpose flour**

¾ teaspoon **baking powder**

Pinch **salt**

Confectioners' sugar, to serve

COMMEMORATION OF ALL THE FAITHFUL DEPARTED (ALL SOULS' DAY)

November 2

On November 2, the Church gathers in prayerful remembrance for All Souls' Day, a solemn feast dedicated to praying for the souls of the faithful departed. Rooted in ancient Christian tradition, this day calls us to lift up our loved ones who have gone before us, entrusting them to God's mercy and the hope of eternal rest.

The Church teaches that some souls, though destined for Heaven, undergo purification in Purgatory—a final cleansing that prepares them for the fullness of God's presence. Our prayers, sacrifices, and Mass offerings on All Souls' Day aid these souls, reflecting the deep communion we share with them in the Body of Christ. This practice has been observed since the early Church and was formally established in the eleventh century by the Benedictine abbot St. Odilo of Cluny.

Throughout the world, All Souls' Day is marked by visits to cemeteries, lighting candles, and offering prayers for the dead. It is a time to remember that death is not the end, but a passage into eternal life.

PAN DE MUERTO

PAN DE MUERTO (OR "BREAD OF the dead") is a homemade bread that is very popular in Mexico. This sweet, aromatic bread, often adorned with bone-shaped dough decorations, is a staple offering during the *Día de los Muertos* festivities, symbolizing the circle of life and remembrance.

1. In a medium-sized bowl, combine the milk, the yeast, 2 tablespoons of flour, and 1 tablespoon of sugar and then cover it and let it rest in a warm place for about 10 minutes.

2. Meanwhile, in a separate bowl, combine the remaining dry ingredients, including the orange zest. Then add the butter and the eggs (one by one) as you mix it all together with a stand mixer or a hand mixer. Add the orange juice, orange blossom water (if using), and vanilla extract.

3. At this point, add the mixture that you set aside, which should be activated at this point. Continue mixing until a slightly elastic dough is formed. It should not be very sticky. This can take up to 20 minutes, depending on the ambient temperature.

4. Grease a bowl, place the dough in the bowl, and cover with a paper towel or slightly damp towel. Roll the dough around so that all sides are greased. Let it rise for one hour in a warm place.

5. Preheat the oven to 350 degrees F. After the dough has doubled in size, cut it into 4 equal-sized pieces. Take three of them and form three smooth balls of equal size. Place them on a pre-greased baking sheet. Cut the last piece into three equal pieces. Roll out 2 thin ropes and one small ball from each piece and cross the ropes over the top of each loaf. Place each small ball at the center of each loaf, pressing down gently. Cover and let rise for 1 hour.

6. Bake for 45 minutes, or until the bread is cooked through. Remove from the oven and brush with melted butter before rolling and coating each piece with white sugar.

INGREDIENTS

SERVES 20

¾ cup **milk**, at room temperature

3 tablespoons **active dry yeast**

4 cups **bread flour**

¾ cup **granulated sugar** plus 1 tablespoon

Zest from one **orange**

¾ cup **butter**

3 **eggs**, at room temperature

2 **egg yolks**

¼ cup **orange juice**

2 tablespoons **orange blossom water**, optional

1 tablespoon **vanilla extract**

1 ½ teaspoons **salt**

¼ cup **butter**, melted, for coating bread after it bakes

1 cup **granulated sugar**, for coating bread after it bakes

Let Us Pray

O Jesus Christ, I acknowledge You as universal King. All that has been made has been created for You. Exercise all Your rights over me. I renew my baptismal vows. I renounce Satan, his pomps and his works; I promise to live as a good Christian. And, in particular do I pledge myself to labor, to the best of my ability, for the triumph of the rights of God and of Your Church.

Divine Heart of Jesus, to You do I offer my poor services, laboring that all hearts may acknowledge Your sacred kingship, and that thus the reign of Your peace be established throughout the whole universe. Amen.

SOLEMNITY OF OUR LORD JESUS CHRIST, KING OF THE UNIVERSE

NOVEMBER, LAST SUNDAY OF EACH LITURGICAL YEAR

As the Church's liturgical year comes to a close, we turn our hearts to the Feast of Christ the King, a solemn reminder that Jesus Christ reigns supreme over all creation. Established in 1925 by Pope Pius XI, this feast was a direct response to the rise of secularism, proclaiming that Christ is not only the King of Heaven but also the rightful Lord of our hearts, homes, and society.

Pope Pius XI, in his encyclical *Quas Primas*, emphasized that Christ's kingship is unlike any earthly rule. His reign is one of truth, love, and mercy, drawing all souls to Himself. He does not rule with force, but with a boundless charity that surpasses all understanding. His dominion extends not through conquest but through the free and loving submission of those who recognize Him as the way, the truth, and the life.

Celebrated on the last Sunday of the liturgical year, the Feast of Christ the King invites us to reflect on whether Christ truly reigns in our lives. Do we give Him authority over our thoughts, actions, and desires? Do we acknowledge His sovereignty in our homes and communities? This feast is a call to enthrone Christ in every aspect of our lives, recognizing that His Kingdom is one of peace, justice, and eternal glory.

As we gather to celebrate this solemnity, may we renew our commitment to serving Christ our King.

CHRIST THE KING POUND CAKE

CREATED IN ENGLAND BACK IN THE early 1700s, pound cake gets its name from the ingredients in the original recipe: one pound of butter, one pound of sugar, one pound of eggs, and one pound of flour. No yeast or other leavening agents were used—whipping the batter gave the cake its rise. As time passed, however, home cooks adjusted the original measurements to make a lighter cake, but the name "pound cake" has remained.

1. Preheat the oven to 325 degrees F. Butter and flour a 10-inch Bundt pan and set aside.

2. Cream the sugar, butter, and shortening until fluffy. Add the eggs, one at a time, beating well after each addition.

3. Sift the dry ingredients together. Add the dry ingredients to the creamed mixture, alternating with the milk. Add the extracts and blend well. Pour the batter into the Bundt pan.

4. Bake for 1 hour and 30 minutes or until a toothpick inserted into the center of the cake comes out clean. Remove from the oven and cool before taking the cake out of the pan.

INGREDIENTS

SERVES 6 TO 8

3 cups **granulated sugar**

½ pound **butter**, at room temperature

½ cup **shortening**

6 **eggs**, at room temperature

3 cups **all-purpose flour**

½ teaspoon **baking powder**

¼ teaspoon **salt**

1 cup **milk**

1 teaspoon **rum extract**

1 teaspoon **coconut extract**, optional

Appendix I

Please photocopy and cut out these cookie and frosting templates for your Jesse Tree cookies.

Jesse Tree Cookie Schedule

Day 1 . . . . Creation (World)

Day 2 . . . . Adam and Eve (Apple)

Day 3 . . . . Noah and the Flood (Ark)

Day 4 . . . . Abraham (Stars)

Day 5 . . . . Isaac (Ram)

Day 6 . . . . Jacob (Ladder)

Day 7 . . . . Joseph (Coat)

Day 8 . . . . Moses (Tablets)

Day 9 . . . . Samuel (Lamp)

Day 10 . . . . David (Harp)

Day 11 . . . Good Shepherd (Shepherd Crook)

Day 12 . . . . Solomon (Crown)

Day 13 . . . . Elijah (Raven)

Day 14 . . . . Isaiah (Tongs)

Day 15 . . . . Ezekiel (Heart)

Day 16 . . . . Nehemiah (Church)

Day 17 . . . . Messiah (Dawn)

Day 18 . . . . New Covenant (River)

Day 19 . . . . Zechariah (Censer)

Day 20 . . . . Gabriel (Angel)

Day 21 . . . . Mary (Lily)

Day 22 . . . . Magnificat (Mary)

Day 23 . . . . John the Baptist (Font)

Day 24 . . . . Joseph (St. Joseph)

Day 25 . . . The Wise Men (Star of Bethlehem)

Day 26 . . . . Baby Jesus (Manger)

ANGEL

APPLE

CROWN

HEART

FONT ICING #1

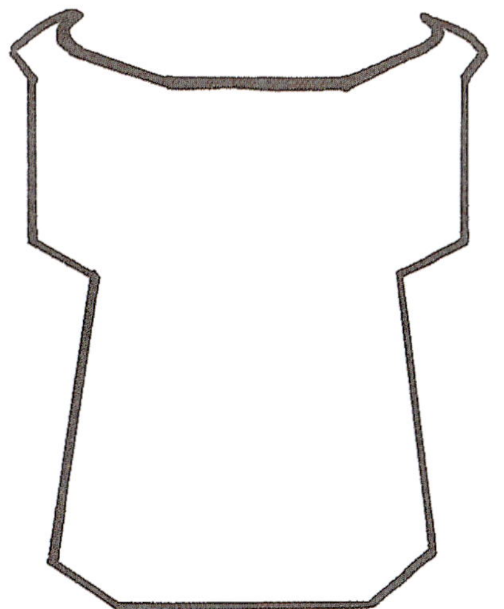

FONT ICING #2

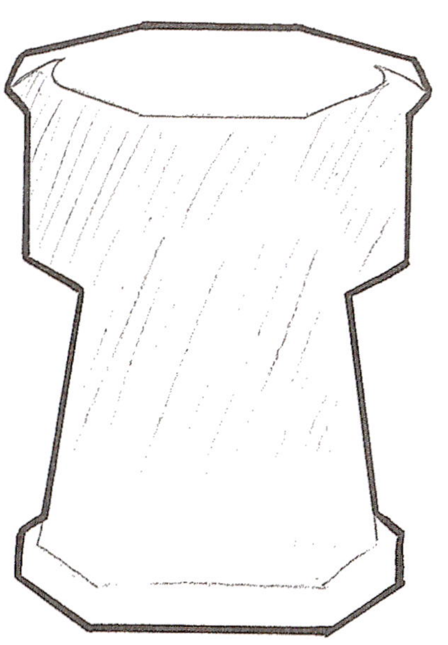

CENSER

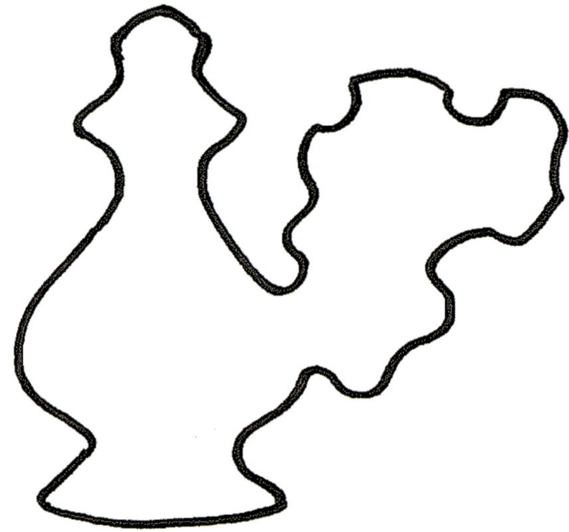

CENSER ICING #1

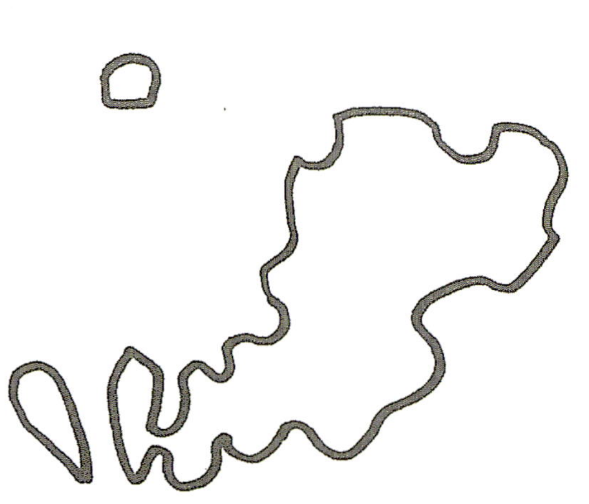

CENSER ICING #2

CHURCH

CHURCH ICING #1

CHURCH ICING #2

COAT

COAT ICING #1

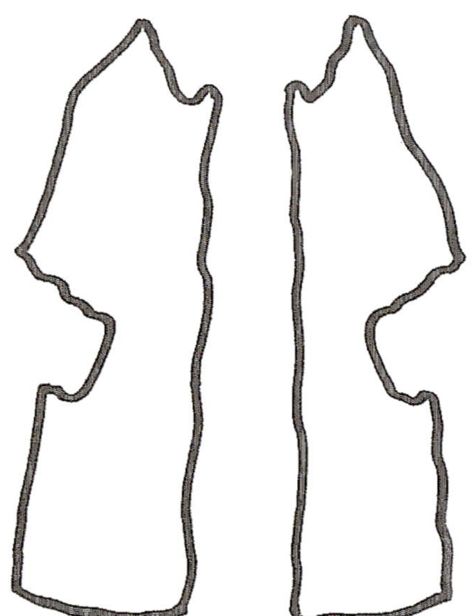

COAT ICING #2

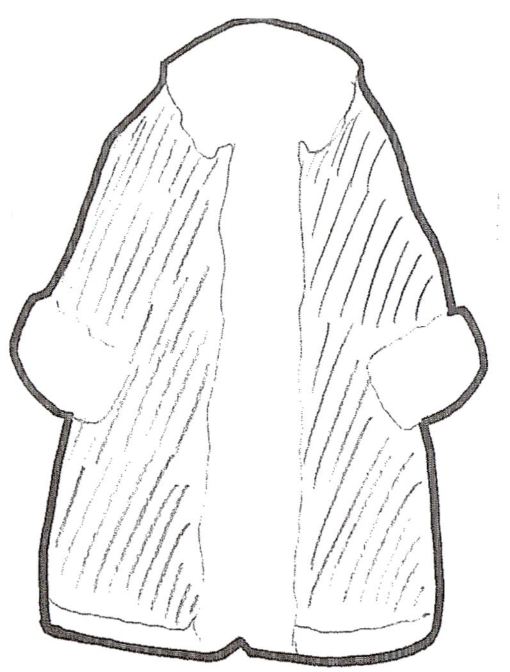

DAWN

DAWN ICING #1

DAWN ICING #2

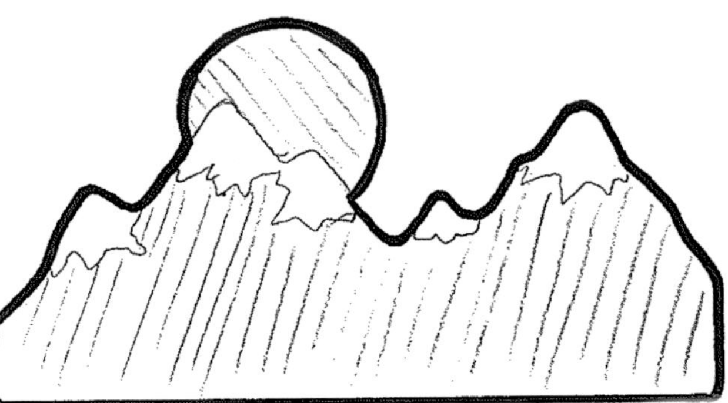

HARP

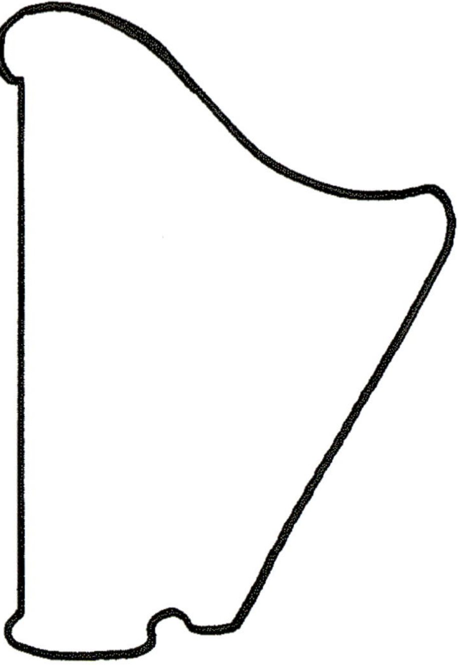

HARP ICING #1

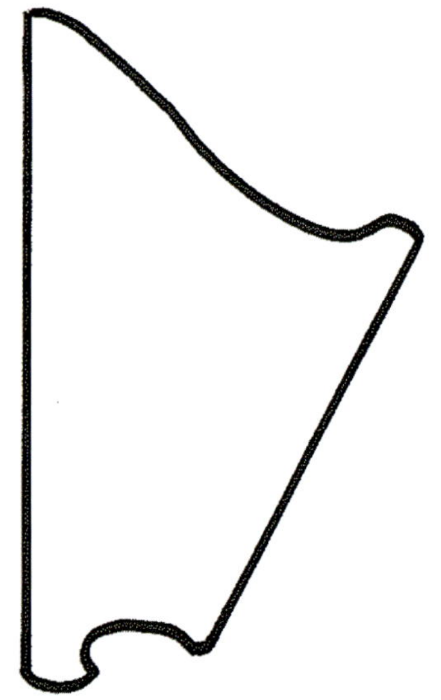

HARP ICING #2

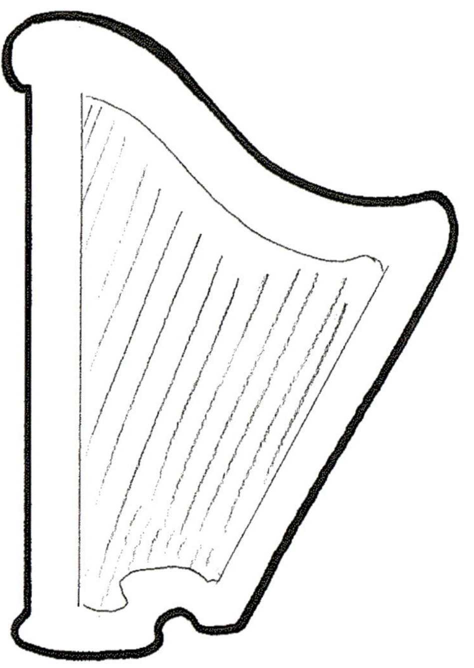

ST. JOSEPH

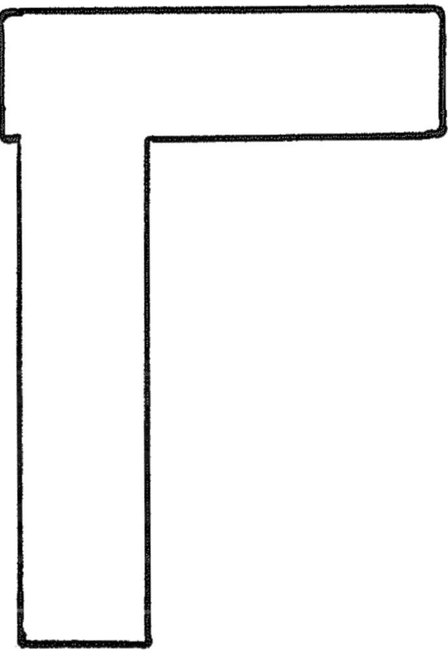

ST. JOSEPH ICING #1

ST. JOSEPH ICING #2

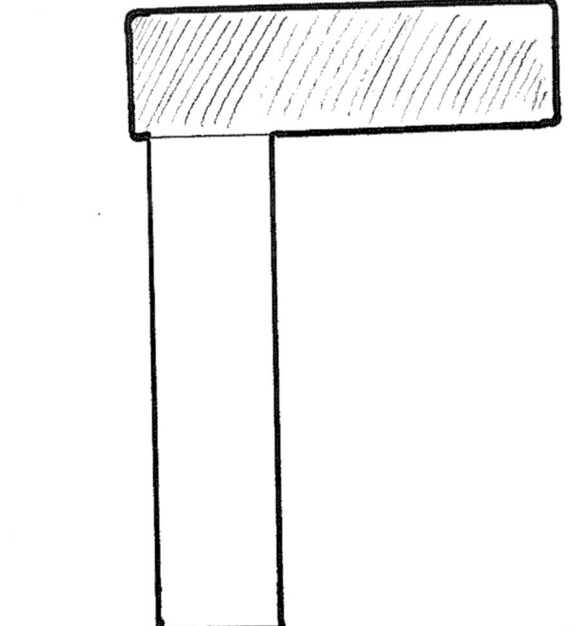

LADDER

LADDER ICING #1

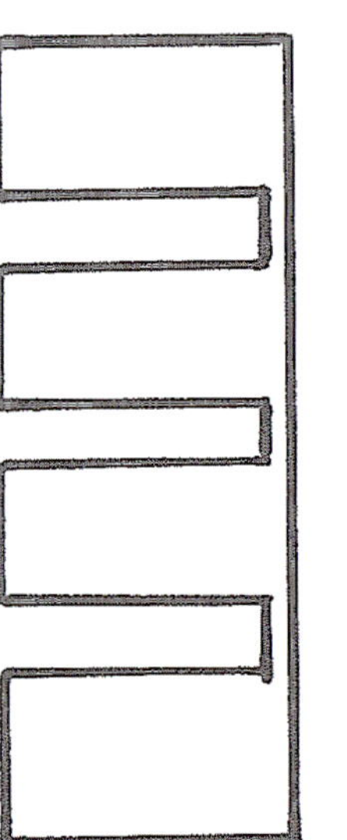

LADDER ICING #2

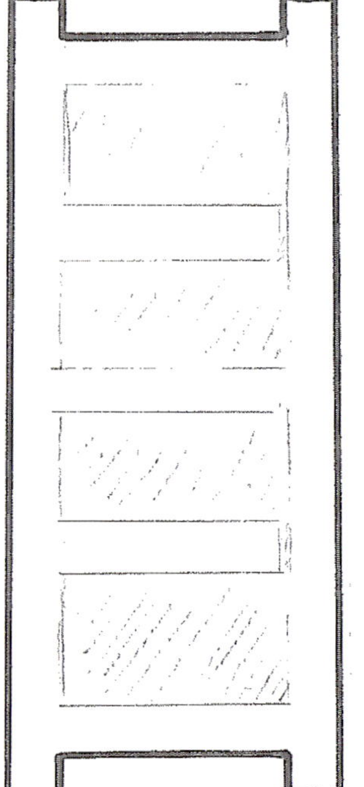

LAMP

LAMP ICING #1

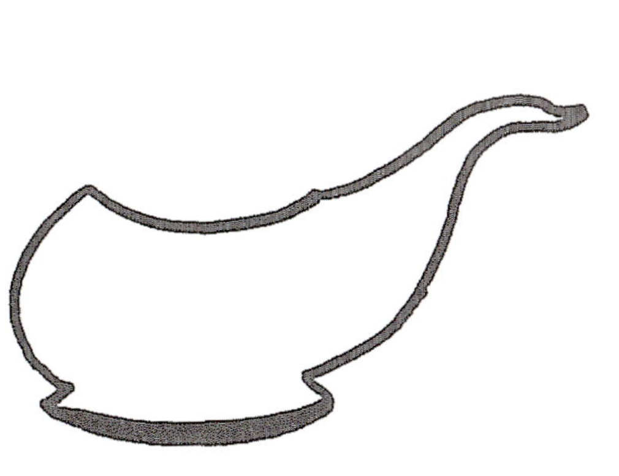

LAMP ICING #2

MANGER

MANGER ICING #1

MANGER ICING #2

ARK

ARK ICING #1

ARK ICING #2

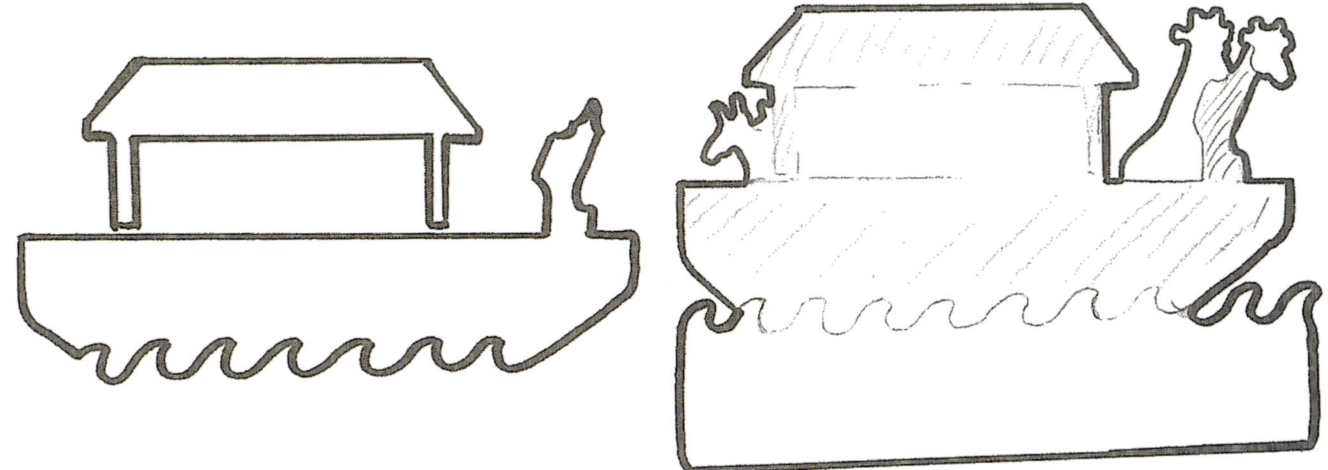

RAM

RAM ICING #1

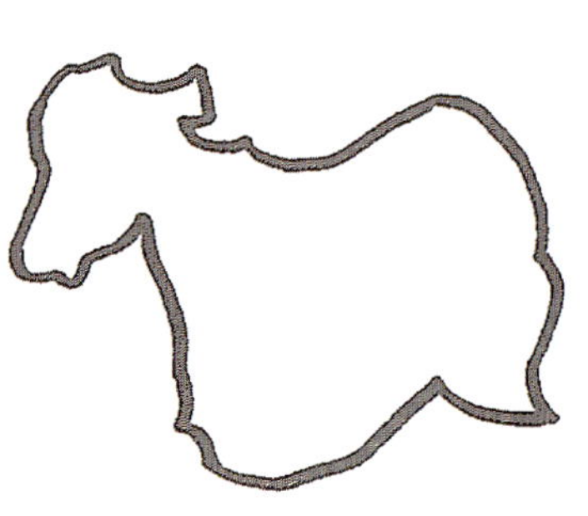

RAM ICING #2

RIVER

RIVER ICING #1

RIVER ICING #2

STARS

STARS ICING #1

STARS ICING #2

TABLETS

TABLETS ICING #1

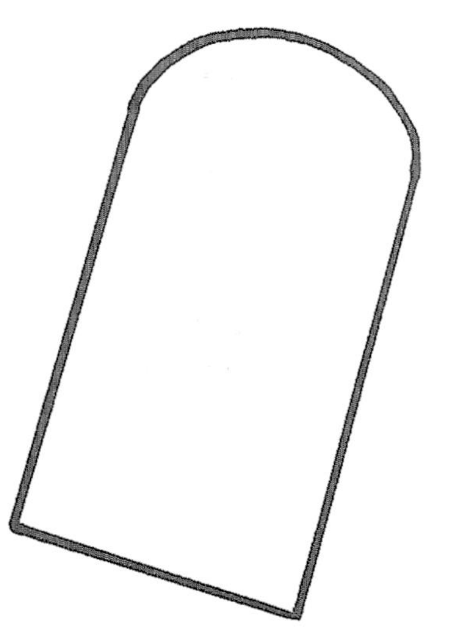

TABLETS ICING #2

TONGS

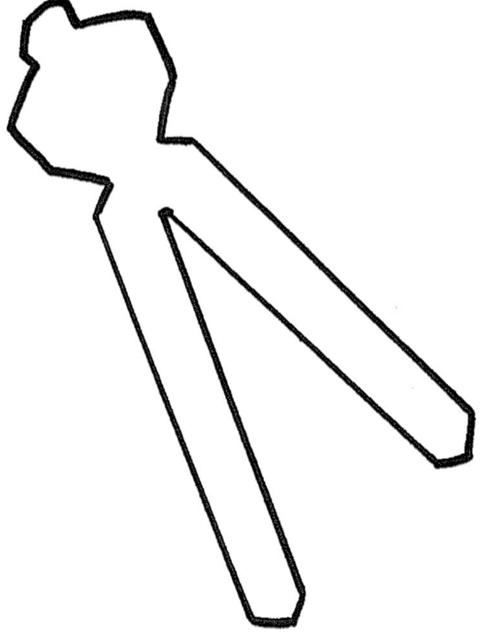

TONGS ICING #1

TONGS ICING #2

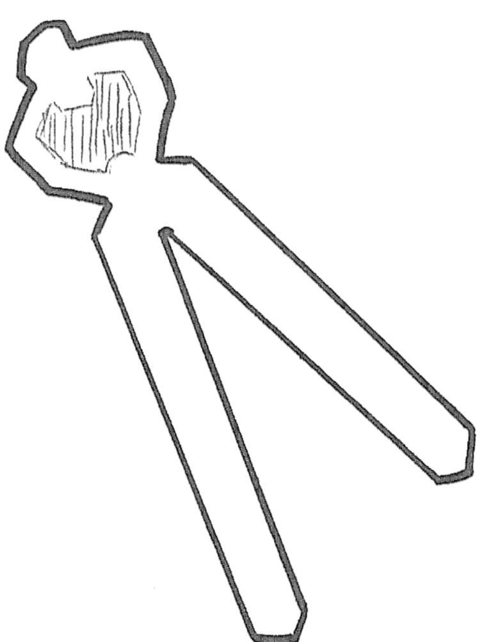

WORLD

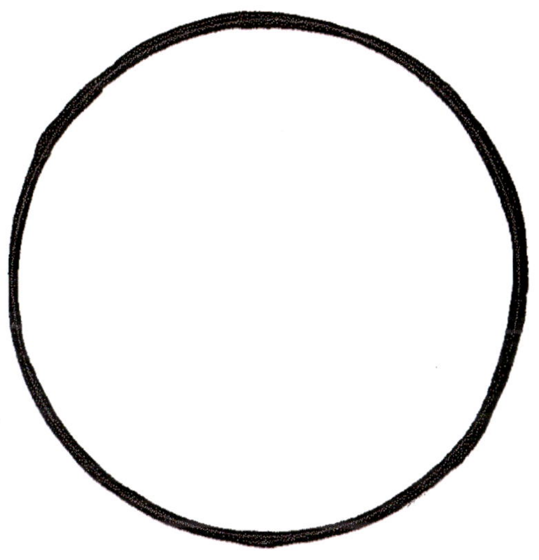

WORLD ICING #1

WORLD ICING #2

LILY

MARY

RAVEN

SHEPHERD CROOK

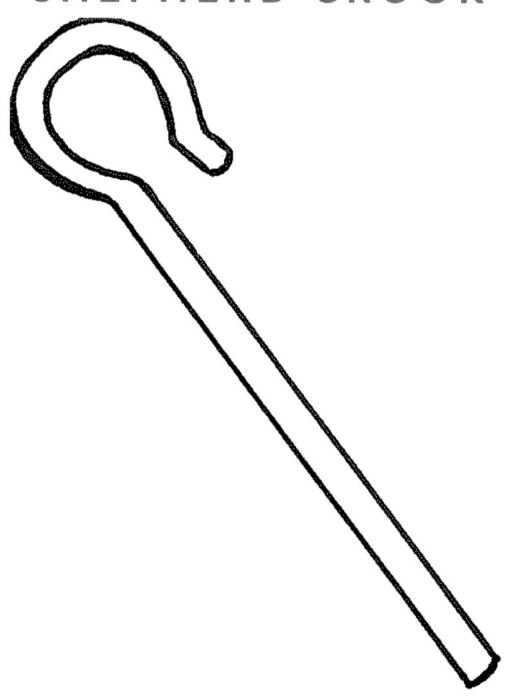

STAR OF BETHLEHEM

Appendix II

Please photocopy and cut out these place cards to dress up your table for your Catholic feast.

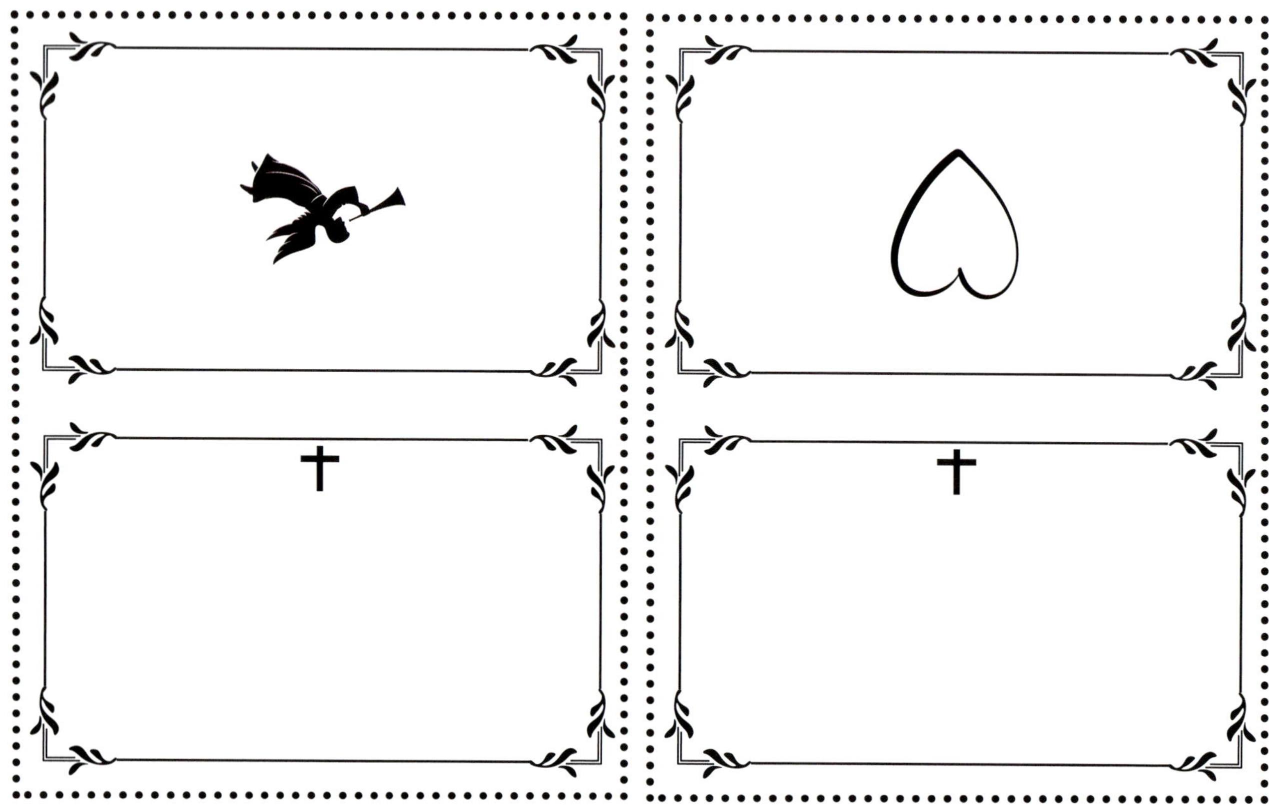

Appendix III

Please photocopy and cut out the St. James Cross for use on the St. James Cake.

Recipe Credits

JESSE TREE COOKIES

Ethel Marbach, *Holy Housewifery Cookbook* (Saint Meinrad, IN: Abbey Press, 1968). Sourced from Catholic Culture, "Catholic Recipe: Jesse Tree Cookies," https://www.catholicculture.org/culture/liturgicalyear/recipes/view.cfm?id=1252.

FRYING PAN COOKIES

Courtesy of Sandy Hanson.

RED-GREEN SALAD

Courtesy of Alexandra Greeley.

SCOTTISH COLLOPS

Courtesy of Anne Parsons, slightly adapted.

ST. BARBARA'S BREAD

Kathy Cutler, *Festive Bread Book* (Woodbury, NY: Barron's Educational Series, Inc., 1982). Sourced from Catholic Culture, "Catholic Recipe: St. Barbara's Bread," https://www.catholicculture.org/culture/liturgicalyear/recipes/view.cfm?id=1115.

BAKLAVA SATCHELS

Feast with the Saints, Baklava Satchels, https://feastwiththesaints.com/how-to-make-baklava-satchels/.

THREE-CHEESE CHICKEN ALFREDO BAKE

Life in the Lofthouse, Three Cheese Chicken Alfredo Bake, https://life-in-the-lofthouse.com/three-cheese-chicken-alfredo-bake/.

CHICKEN MOLE

Courtesy of Rita Steininger, slightly adapted.

ST. LUCIA BUNS

P.J. Hamel, King Arthur Baking Company, St. Lucia Buns, https://www.kingarthurbaking.com/recipes/st-lucia-buns-recipe.

HOMEMADE EGGNOG

Courtesy of G. Shepherd.

SWEET-SAVORY FISH SOUP

Courtesy of G. Shepherd.

EASY BAKED HAM WITH MAPLE AND BROWN SUGAR GLAZE

Jason Norris, Recipe Teacher, Easy Baked Ham with Maple and Brown Sugar Glaze, https://recipeteacher.com/easy-baked-ham-with-maple-and-brown-sugar-glaze/.

MASHED SWEET POTATOES

Sara Welch, Dinner at the Zoo, Mashed Sweet Potatoes, https://www.dinneratthezoo.com/mashed-sweet-potatoes/.

GREEN BEANS WITH PISTACHIOS AND RAISINS

Courtesy of Alexandra Greeley.

CHRISTMAS DINNER ROLLS WITH BROWN BUTTER AND ROSEMARY

Paula Rhodes, Salad in a Jar, Brown Butter Rosemary Rolls (Shaped as a Wreath), https://saladinajar.com/recipes/bread/savory-loaves-and-rolls/brown-butter-and-rosemary-dinner-rolls-dressed-up-for-christmas/.

GAUDETE MINCEMEAT PIES

Kristen Einertson and Tessa Muench, All the Household, Gaudete Mincemeat Pies, https://allthehousehold.com/gaudete-mincemeat-pies/.

CRISPY GINGER COOKIES

Jennifer Segal, Once Upon a Chef, Crispy Ginger Cookies, https://www.onceuponachef. com/recipes/crispy-ginger-cookies.html (Adapted from *Stars Desserts* by Emily Luchetti).

ST. JOHN'S WINE (MULLED WINE)

Florence Berger, *Cooking for Christ* (National Catholic Rural Life Conference, 1949, 1999). Sourced from Catholic Culture, "Catholic Recipe: St. John's Wine (Mulled Wine)," https:// www.catholicculture.org/culture/liturgicalyear/ recipes/view.cfm?id=193.

SPINACH-LENTIL SOUP

Courtesy of G. Shepherd.

LADYFINGERS

King Arthur Test Kitchen, King Arthur Baking Company, Ladyfingers, https://www. kingarthurbaking.com/recipes/ladyfingers-recipe.

ROSCA DE REYES THREE KING'S CAKE

Susan Reid, King Arthur Baking Company, Three Kings Cake (Rosca de Reyes), https:// www.kingarthurbaking.com/recipes/ three-kings-cake-rosca-de-reyes-recipe.

SCALLOP SHELL SALAD WITH SARDINES

Courtesy of Alexandra Greeley.

CANDLEMAS CRÊPES

Barbara Stein, *Catholic Cuisine*, "Candlemas Crepes," https://catholiccuisine.blogspot. com/2009/02/candlemas-crepes.html.

EMBER DAY SHRIMP TEMPURA

Courtesy of Catholic All Year

VALENTINE'S DAY CAKE

Courtesy of Anne Parson.

BUTTERMILK PANCAKES

Jessica Gordon, *Catholic Cuisine*, "Shrove Tuesday—Pancake Day!," https:// catholiccuisine.blogspot.com/2011/03/shrove-tuesday-pancake-day.html.

GEORGANN'S SPINACH QUICHE

Courtesy of Ann Parsons, adapted by G. Shepherd.

BEEF AND GUINNESS PIE

Elaine Lemm, The Spruce Eats, Beef and Guinness Pie, https://www.thespruceeats.com/ beef-and-guinness-pie-recipe-435724, adapted by G. Shepherd.

ZEPPOLE DI SAN GIUSEPPE

Christina Conte, Christina's Cucina, Zeppole di San Giuseppe (St. Joseph's Day Traditional Italian Pastries), https://www.christinascucina. com/zeppole-di-san-giuseppe-st-josephs-day-traditional-italian-pastries/.

FEAST OF THE ANNUNCIATION SWEDISH WAFFLES

Katherine Burton and Helmut Ripperger, *Feast Day Cookbook* (New York: David McKay Company, Inc., 1951). Sourced from Catholic Culture, "Catholic Recipe: Swedish Waffles," https://www.catholicculture.org/culture/ liturgicalyear/recipes/view.cfm?id=37.

FIG-ARUGULA SALAD WITH GOAT CHEESE

Courtesy of Alexandra Greeley and Christine Butters.

UNLEAVENED BREAD OR MATZO

Annette Reeder, The Biblical Nutritionist, "Unleavened Bread Recipe—How to Make an Israeli Classic," https://thebiblicalnutritionist. com/how-to-make-unleavened-bread-recipe/.

CREAMY CORN CHOWDER WITH SHRIMP

Courtesy of Alexandra Greeley and Sonia Carrero.

STUFFED GRAPE LEAVES

Courtesy of G. Shepherd.

RESURRECTION ROLLS

Christy Denney, The Girl Who Ate Everything, Empty Tomb Rolls, https://www.the-girl-who-ate-everything.com/empty-tomb-rolls/.

DEVILED EGGS

Tested by Susan Holleran and Kathie Sachs.

DATES STUFFED WITH PISTACHIOS

Courtesy of Alexandra Greeley and Christine Butters.

RACHEL'S ROAST LAMB

Courtesy of Anne Parsons.

CREAMY MASHED POTATOES

Courtesy of Mary K. Grant.

FRESH ASPARAGUS WITH RED PEPPERS, ALMONDS, AND OLIVES

Courtesy of Alexandra Greeley. Tested by Susan Holleran and Katherine Sachs.

EASY BUTTERMILK DROP BISCUITS

Tiffany Dahle, Peanut Blossom, Easy Buttermilk Drop Biscuits, https://www.peanutblossom.com/blog/buttermilk-drop-biscuits/.

PASHKA

Courtesy of Veronica Ciregna.

DIVINE MERCY SHORTCAKE

Barbara Stein, Catholic Mom, "Bake a Divine Mercy Shortcake," https://www.catholicmom.com/articles/bake-a-divine-mercy-shortcake.

CHICKEN SALAD SANDWICH

Courtesy of Christine Butters and Alexandra Greeley.

PENTECOST CAKE

Helen McLoughlin, *Family Customs: Easter to Pentecost* (Collegeville, MN: The Liturgical Press, 1956). Sourced from Catholic Culture, "Catholic Recipe: Pentecost Cake," https://www.catholicculture.org/culture/liturgicalyear/recipes/view.cfm?id=273.

GOD CAKES

Katherine Burton and Helmut Ripperger, *Feast Day Cookbook* (New York: David McKay Company, Inc., 1951). Sourced from Catholic Culture, "Catholic Recipe: God Cakes," https://www.catholicculture.org/culture/liturgicalyear/recipes/view.cfm?id=6.

CINNAMON CROWN CAKE

Jennifer McHenry, Bake or Break, Cinnamon Crown Cake, https://bakeorbreak.com/2007/11/cinnamon-crown-cake/.

CARNE VINHO DE ALHOS

Mary Machado, *Catholic Cuisine*, "Portuguese Dish for Our Lady of Fatima," https://catholiccuisine.blogspot.com/2008/05/portuguese-dish-for-our-lady-of-fatima.html.

CRÈME BRÛLÉE

Feast with the Saints, Crème Brûlée, https://feastwiththesaints.com/how-to-make-creme-brulee/.

ITALIAN PIZZELLE COOKIES

Angela Allison, This Italian Kitchen, Pizzelle Cookies (Traditional Italian Waffle Cookies), https://thisitaliankitchen.com/pizzelle-cookies/.

PISTACHIO ROSEWATER COOKIES

Analida Braeger, Analida Ethnic Spoon, Pistachio Rosewater Cookies, https://ethnicspoon.com/pistachio-rosewater-cookies/.

HONEY CAKE

Feast with the Saints, Honey Cake, https://feastwiththesaints.com/how-to-make-honey-cake/.

CRESPILLOS

Alicia Bustos, *Cocina Inteligente* (Pamplona: Eunsa, 2004). Sourced from OpusDei.org, "Dora del Hoyo," https://opusdei.org/en/article/recipe-for-crespillos/.

FILLET OF FLOUNDER IN TOMATO SAUCE

Katherine Burton and Helmut Ripperger, *Feast Day Cookbook* (New York: David McKay Company, Inc., 1951). Sourced from Catholic Culture, "Catholic Recipe: Fillet of Flounder in Tomato Sauce," https://www.catholicculture.org/culture/liturgicalyear/recipes/view.cfm?id=81.

GOAN RICE PULAO

Courtesy of Joe Fernandes.

SPANAKOPITA

Feast with the Saints, Spanakopita, https://feastwiththesaints.com/07/25/saint-christopher/#spanakopita-recipe.

TARTA DE SANTIAGO (SPANISH ALMOND CAKE OR ST. JAMES CAKE)

Lauren Aloise, Spanish Sabores, Spanish Almond Cake (Tarta de Santiago Recipe), https://spanishsabores.com/tarta-de-santiago-recipe-spanish-almond-cake/.

PIEROGI

Feast with the Saints, Pierogi, https://feastwiththesaints.com/08/14/saint-maximilian-kolbe/#pierogi-recipe.

ASSUMPTA SALAD

Victor Antoine d'Avila-Latourrette, *Twelve Months of Monastery Salads: 200 Divine Recipes for All Seasons* (Harvard Common Press, 2006). Sourced from Catholic Culture, "Catholic Recipe: Assumpta Salad," https://www.catholicculture.org/culture/liturgicalyear/recipes/view.cfm?id=1689.

CEVICHE

Courtesy of Fr. Hezekias Carnazzo

BARTLEMAS BEEF

Julia Jones and Barbara Deer, *A Calendar of Feasts, Cattern Cakes and Lace* (Dorling Kindersley, 1987). Sourced from Meres & Meadows Messenger. Adapted by G. Shepherd.

NAAN FLATBREAD

Feast with the Saints, Naan Flatbread, https://feastwiththesaints.com/09/05/saint-teresa-of-calcutta/#naan-recipe.

HOT CROSS BUNS

P.J. Hamel, King Arthur Baking Company, Easy Hot Cross Buns, https://www.kingarthurbaking.com/recipes/easy-hot-cross-buns-recipe.

ST. MATTHEW SILVER DOLLAR PANCAKES

Courtesy of Catholic All Year

MICHAELMAS PIE

Catholic Culture, "Catholic Recipe: Michaelmas Pie," https://www.catholicculture.org/culture/liturgicalyear/recipes/view.cfm?id=1478.

ANGEL DELIGHT

Courtesy of Wanda Beth Atkinson via Kathleen Marshall.

POOR MAN'S CAKE

Barbara Stein, *Catholic Cuisine*, "Poor Man's Cake for St. Francis of Assisi," https://catholiccuisine.blogspot.com/2010/10/poor-mans-cake-for-st-francis-of-assisi.html.

KREMÓWKA PAPIESKA

Feast with the Saints, Kremówka Papieska, https://feastwiththesaints.com/how-to-make-kremowka-papieska/.

EGYPTIAN FALAFEL

Amira's Pantry, Egyptian Falafel, https://amiraspantry.com/falafel/, adapted.

ALL SAINTS' DAY COOKIES (OSSA DEI MORTI)

Deborah Mele, Italian Food Forever, All Saints Day Cookies—Ossa dei Morti, https://italianfoodforever.com/2019/11/all-saints-day-cookies-ossa-dei-morti/.

PAN DE MUERTO

Charbel Barker, My Latina Table, Authentic Mexican Pan de Muerto, https://www.mylatinatable.com/authentic-mexican-pan-de-muerto-recipe/.

CHRIST THE KING POUND CAKE

Ashley Tumlin Wallace, Anglican Compass, Christ the King Pound Cake, https://anglicancompass.com/the-liturgical-home-the-feast-of-christ-the-king/.

Image Credits

Cover images:

Rosary with cross drawn (1415944294), image derived from Luka / stock.adobe.com

One line drawing praying (1073241116), image derived from katsumatakun / stock.adobe.com

Bell pepper (744797228), image derived from artisttop / stock.adobe.com

Wine glasses (595533021), image derived from conartline / stock.adobe.com

Different veggies (267716517), image derived from ursulamea / stock.adobe.com

Cutlery continuous (906547860), image derived from isdiyono / stock.adobe.com

Old canvas texture (103853186), image derived from Dmytro Synelnychenko / stock.adobe.com

White paper texture (248310678), image derived from natrot / stock.adobe.com

Table AI image created by Updatefordesign Studio

Food Photography:

Melissa Lew

Interior images (given in order of appearance):

Jesse Tree by Absolon Stumme, National Museum in Warsaw, commons.Wikimedia.org, Public Domain.

O Antiphons, Antiphonarium pro Ecclesia Einsidlensi folio 015r "Ô Antiphonen," commons.Wikimedia.org, Public Domain.

A Christmas Carol in Lucerne by Hans Bachmann, commons.Wikimedia.org, Public Domain.

St. Andrew by Peter Paul Rubens, Museo del Prado, commons.Wikimedia.org, Public Domain.

St. Barbara by Giovanni Antonio Boltraffio, Gemäldegalerie Berlin, commons.Wikimedia.org, Public Domain.

St. Nicholas by Jean Bourdichon, in *Les Grandes Heures d'Anne de Bretagne*, commons.Wikimedia.org, Public Domain.

Immaculate Conception by Giovanni Battista Tiepolo, Museo del Prado, commons.Wikimedia.org, Public Domain.

Our Lady of Gaudalupe, Basilica of Our Lady of Guadalupe, commons.Wikimedia.org, Public Domain.

St. Lucy by Benvenuto Tisi, Capitoline Museums, commons.Wikimedia.org, Public Domain.

Children by the Christmas Tree by Leopold Graf von Kalckreuth, National Museum in Warsaw, commons.Wikimedia.org, Public Domain.

The Nativity by John Singleton Copley (KEAC3R), alamy.com / Historic Collection.

Chopped fresh dill with wooden spoon (2595538701), shutterstock.com / kateryna labyk.

Garlic crushed and garlic press (177385334), shutterstock.com / ffolas.

Pile of Chopped Red Pepper on Cutting Board (669987964), shutterstock.com / beast01.

Raw scallop on a wooden board (1936515868), shutterstock.com / Rainer Plendl.

Saint John the Evangelist by Domenichino, National Gallery, London, commons.Wikimedia.org, Public Domain.

The Virgin with the Lilies by William-Adolphe Bouguereau, Private collection, commons.Wikimedia.org, Public Domain.

Epiphany by Francisco Herrera the Elder, Museu Nacional d'Art de Catalunya, commons.Wikimedia.org, Public Domain.

The Baptism of Christ by José Ferraz de Almeida Júnior, Pinacoteca de São Paulo, commons.Wikimedia.org, Public Domain.

Presentation in the Temple by Philippe de Champaigne, Royal Museums of Fine Arts of Belgium, commons.Wikimedia.org, Public Domain.

St. Paul Miki by Theophilia.

Saint Valentine Blesses, Crowns the Marriage of a Girl and a Boy (569225950), stock.adobe.com / Vasilii.

Confession by Pietro Antonio Novelli, commons.Wikimedia.org, Public Domain.

Ash Wednesday by Julian Fałat, Private collection, commons.Wikimedia.org, Public Domain.

St. Patrick, Church of the Assumption, commons.Wikimedia.org / CC3 Andreas F. Borchert.

Saint Joseph and the Christ Child by Bartolomé Esteban Murillo, John and Mable Ringling Museum of Art, commons.Wikimedia.org, Public Domain.

The Annunciation by Luca Giordano, Metropolitan Museum of Art, commons.Wikimedia.org, Public Domain.

L'Entrée du Christ à Jérusalem by Peter Paul Rubens, Musée des Beaux-Arts de Dijon, commons.Wikimedia.org, Public Domain.

Last Supper by Leonardo da Vinci, Santa Maria delle Grazie, commons.Wikimedia.org, Public Domain.

Christ Crucified by Diego Velázquez, Museo del Prado, commons. Wikimedia.org, Public Domain.

Resurrection of Christ by Giovanni Bellini, Gemäldegalerie Berlin, commons.Wikimedia.org, Public Domain.

Christ's Appearance to Mary Magdalene after the Resurrection by Alexander Andreyevich Ivanov, Russian Museum, commons. Wikimedia.org, Public Domain.

The Resurrection of Christ with SS. Leonard of Noblac and Lucia by Giovanni Antonio Boltraffio and Marco d'Oggiono, Gemäldegalerie Berlin, commons.Wikimedia.org, Public Domain.

Divine Mercy by Eugeniusz Kazimirowski, Divine Mercy Sanctuary in Vilnius, commons.Wikimedia.org, Public Domain.

Ascension by John Singleton Copley, Museum of Fine Arts Boston, commons.Wikimedia.org, Public Domain.

Pentecost by El Greco (2A4MWGC), Museo del Prado, alamy. com / incamerastock.

Adoration of the Trinity by Albrecht Dürer, Kunsthistorisches Museum, commons.Wikimedia.org, Public Domain.

Crowning of Mary by Av8erPhotography (93811414), stock. adobe.com / Av8erPhotography.

Our Lady of Fatima by José Ferreira Thedim, Chapel of the Apparitions, commons.Wikimedia.org, Public Domain.

St. Joan by Jan Styka, commons.Wikimedia.org, Public Domain.

Corpus Christi Procession with Pope Gregory XVI in the Vatican by Ferdinando Cavalleri, commons.Wikimedia.org, Public Domain.

L'Apparition du Sacré-Coeur à sainte Marguerite-Marie by Unidentified painter, Saint-Charles-Borromée Church (Charlesbourg), commons.Wikimedia.org, Public Domain.

St. John the Baptist from the *Adoration of the Lamb* by Jan Van Eyck, St. Bavo's Cathedral, commons.Wikimedia.org, Public Domain.

St. Josemaría Escrivá from *Oficina de Información de la Prelatura del Opus Dei en España*, commons.Wikimedia.org / CC2 Opus Dei Communications Office.

Saint Paul by Peter Paul Rubens, Private collection, commons. Wikimedia.org, Public Domain.

St. Thomas by Peter Paul Rubens, Museo del Prado, commons. Wikimedia.org, Public Domain.

Saint Christopher Carrying the Christ Child by Hieronymus Bosch, Museum Boijmans Van Beuningen, commons.Wikimedia. org, Public Domain.

St. James the Apostle by Peter Paul Rubens, Museo del Prado, commons.Wikimedia.org, Public Domain.

Maximilian Kolbe in 1936, commons.Wikimedia.org, Public Domain.

La Asunción de la Virgen by Juan Martín Cabezalero, Museo del Prado, commons.Wikimedia.org, Public Domain.

St. Rose of Lima by Claudio Coello, Museo del Prado, commons. Wikimedia.org, Public Domain.

St. Bartholomew by Peter Paul Rubens, Museo del Prado, commons.Wikimedia.org, Public Domain.

St. Mother Teresa (116565201), stock.adobe.com / dannywilde.

Saint Helena by Giovanni Battista Cima da Conegliano, National Gallery of Art, commons.Wikimedia.org, Public Domain.

The Evangelist Matthew, Greece, Athos, Hilandar Monastery, commons.Wikimedia.org, Public Domain.

The Three Archangels with Tobias by Francesco Botticini, Uffizi Galleries, commons.Wikimedia.org, Public Domain.

The Guardian Angel by Pietro da Cortona, Galleria Nazionale d'Arte Antica, commons.Wikimedia.org, Public Domain.

Saint Francis of Assisi by Philip Fruytiers, Royal Museum of Fine Arts Antwerp, commons.Wikimedia.org, Public Domain.

St. John Paul II, commons.Wikimedia.org / CC3 Gregorini Demetrio.

St. Simon by Peter Paul Rubens, Museo del Prado, commons. Wikimedia.org, Public Domain.

Painting with Saints, Guardian Angels church, commons. Wikimedia.org / CC4 Syrio.

An Angel Frees the Souls of Purgatory by Ludovico Carracci, Pinacoteca Vaticana, commons.Wikimedia.org, Public Domain.

Polyptych of Earthly Vanities and Heavenly Redemption by Hans Memling, Musée des Beaux-Arts de Strasbourg, commons. Wikimedia.org, Public Domain.

Other Licensed Elements:
1436862449 (stock.adobe.com) Anca (c)

Elements used in the place cards:
AdobeStock_991112526
AdobeStock_1341810656
AdobeStock_1230086696
AdobeStock_585746947
AdobeStock_250226577
AdobeStock_444998334
AdobeStock_1136909405
AdobeStock_248042211

Cross_Santiago, commons.Wikimedia.org, Public Domain.

Feast Index

Index

Sophia Institute

Sophia Institute is a nonprofit institution that seeks to nurture the spiritual, moral, and cultural life of souls and to spread the Gospel of Christ in conformity with the authentic teachings of the Roman Catholic Church.

Sophia Institute Press fulfills this mission by offering translations, reprints, and new publications that afford readers a rich source of the enduring wisdom of mankind.

Sophia Institute also operates the popular online resource CatholicExchange.com. Catholic Exchange provides world news from a Catholic perspective as well as daily devotionals and articles that will help readers to grow in holiness and live a life consistent with the teachings of the Church.

In 2013, Sophia Institute launched Sophia Institute for Teachers to renew and rebuild Catholic culture through service to Catholic education. With the goal of nurturing the spiritual, moral, and cultural life of souls, and an abiding respect for the role and work of teachers, we strive to provide materials and programs that are at once enlightening to the mind and ennobling to the heart; faithful and complete, as well as useful and practical.

Sophia Institute gratefully recognizes the Solidarity Association for preserving and encouraging the growth of our apostolate over the course of many years. Without their generous and timely support, this book would not be in your hands.

www.SophiaInstitute.com
www.CatholicExchange.com
www.SophiaTeachers.org